CROSSROADS

Living A Soul Inspired Life

Katye Anna

Published by:
Katye Anna SoulWorks
7162 Kopp Rd Spring Grove PA
www.katyeanna.com

ISBN: 978-0-692-70349-6
Library of Congress Control Number:

Cover design, and typesetting by Ranilo Cabo
Proofreader: George Mummert

Printed in the United States of America

CROSSROADS

Living A Soul Inspired Life

Dedications

I dedicate this book to God, my soul and the angels. I'm beyond grateful for the love and support of my daughter Kathy, son Lloyd, Leslie, my grandchildren, Kayla, Josh, Kourtney, Hunter, Shae-Lynn, my brother George and my mother, Kathryn Mummert. I want to thank my students and clients, you continue to inspire me and make me a better teacher. I thank Anna, Allan Sethius, Johnny and the world of spirit for your guidance, love and support. I also want to thank the many people I share strong soul contracts with. Thank you for the life lessons. Thank you for being that which I asked you to be so I that I can be that which I need to be.

Table of Contents

Introduction

I'm sitting here writing during a snowstorm. As I look out at the snow I started thinking about the many twists and turns my life has taken. I know without a doubt that I AM who I was born to be. Many of my students have asked me how I became the person I am today, meaning a teacher of soul and a modern day mystic who knows she walks as one with God.

As I look back on my life I can clearly see there was a path for me to follow. This path was created by my soul before I was born. Of course, this path didn't light up like a Christmas tree. The path was much more subtle than that, but it was there none the less.

I'm not going to write about my childhood or even the first thirty years of my life. Like most people I had been humanized. Like many people I had experiences that were not in alignment with love. These experiences can rock the world of the little incarnated child. I know they rocked mine. When I was a little girl I could see beings of light, they were my friends. By the age of ten, seeing beings of light (angels) and the world of spirit was pushed to the confines of my mind, but God, as I understood him, was always there, listening, caring and letting me know I was not alone.

I call myself a modern day mystic.

In the truest sense of the word a mystic seeks union with God. In ages past a mystic would spend years under the guidance of a spiritual teacher. The mystic would learn to know God in every activity and experience. Many mystics would cloister themselves off from the world believing that the world would prevent them from fully being one with God. The modern day mystic does not live a life cloistered away from the world.

Without even knowing it perhaps life itself is the journey of the modern day mystic. Experiencing God through all activities and experiences while cloistered away, is one thing, but to experience God in all our activities and experiences through our everyday lives is another. The many twists and turns our lives take and the critical choice points we each encounter along the way - perhaps this is the path of the modern day mystic.

I believe it is.

To know God during the times of great sorrow and challenges as well as times of great joy and happiness is the path of the modern day mystic.

I realize now that I have always been a mystic. At the core of my being was always this "energy" pulling me on an unseen path. I now know this "energy" was my soul.

My desire to be one with God was experienced throughout my life. I always loved God. My concept of God was simple, God was loving. God was. For the first forty years of my life I had a very limited view of God. For the first forty years of my life I experienced God as having male energy. I knew God heard me when I talked to him and I could "feel" God talking back to me. As a child one way I experienced God was through nature. My grandmother's garden was a place where I heard God speak to me via the plant life that was all around. Every rose had a message for me as did the grapes hanging in the grape arbor. The smell of the grapes is still etched upon my memory. I heard God through the butterflies and the birds. No matter what was going on in my life I knew God was to be found in my grandmother's garden, in nature, and in the wind. God spoke to me through the trees and still does. I am still in awe when God speaks to me through the wind. As a child, I didn't do anything to connect with God. God was always there, many times when humans weren't.

I could feel God IN me.

Even now I can't explain this, but I knew that God was not out there somewhere, but he was always close by, as close as my breath. God was my resting place. God was my hiding place. God was. As a child I also experienced God through Jesus. Again, my experience of Jesus was simple. Jesus walked the path of love and somehow this has always been the core teaching I embraced about Jesus.

The path of love, this was the path for me. As a child and even as a young adult much of what I experienced about God or life wasn't a conscious process. Today, sitting here writing, my connection with God and what I create in my life, for the most part, is conscious. Tears well up in my eyes as I'm writing because I feel God's presence stirring me to write my story.

Feeling God's presence is all consuming. I take deep breaths and enter into the feelings. Consciously entering into God via my feelings takes everything to a heightened state of oneness.

In writing my story I believe that my reader will start identifying with the path of the mystic through their own life.

I believe at our core we all seek union with that which has created us.

I invite you to begin reflecting on your own life as you read my words. At the end of each chapter I have included a key point section and a reflection section. Perhaps you will begin to identify what I call critical choice points and initiations in your own life. I believe these critical choice points occur when our soul is inviting us to take a step onto a different path.

I refer to critical choice points as a time in one's life when we come to a crossroad. The choice we make will determine the path one takes for learning soul lessons. I believe there are no wrong paths. Different paths simply offer different experiences. I believe we each have six to eight critical choice points during our lives.

During our lives we also go through many stages of initiations and activations which go unnoticed by most personalities. I share several of mine in hopes that you will understand that you and I are not so different.

I believe we all are mystics at heart. When you begin to see your life via the lens of your inner mystic your life and your experiences, perhaps, will begin to make sense.

I share my journey with you that you too may experience walking as one with God. Blessings, Katye Anna

Part One

The Journey

CHAPTER ONE

A Critical Choice Point

It's very easy for me, as I look back, to see a major critical choice point I experienced in my life. I was 29 years old. I was living a very unconscious life. By this I mean old outdated beliefs and patterns had guided my life and my life choices. The path I had set out on, as a child, was the path of the victim. Of course I had no conscious understanding of this. The majority of my life lessons were being learned by the initiations of fire and fear. My vibrational signature unbeknownst to me was sending out messages of victim.

Everyone has a vibrational signature. This vibrational signature holds old outdated beliefs and patterns. Your personality's vibrational signature was created between birth and six years old based on the vibrational signatures of those around you and childhood experiences. To understand what messages your vibrational signature is sending out at any time in your life think about what your life was like.

Clearly up until my thirtieth birthday I was creating my experiences, unconsciously and via victim energy. The lessons of the victim are all about getting the personality to move beyond fear and embrace their own power. Childhood wounding and experiences set me on a path of shutting down and allowing life to *happen* to me instead of being the *creative force* in my own life I was born to be. I believe this is true for many people.

As children we create our childhood experiences based on the core vibrational signature of the tribe. I view childhood itself as a core initiation. These initiations in the form of life experiences can rock the world of a child. As children we make agreements and everything we experience is formed from those agreements. Nothing enters your life without you having first made an agreement to allow it to do so. Many of the agreements we make as children shape how we will view the world and ourselves until, or if, we make a new agreement. The world and people can only show up in our lives in the way we have agreed to allow them in.

Traditionally when we first move away from our tribe we continue to create life experiences via the core vibrational signature of our tribe. As we grow and mature we begin to question the old outdated beliefs of our tribe and naturally release them, however many of the core beliefs you agreed to from birth to six years old continue to govern your life today.

I never moved away from home, therefore I did not question anything. I understand now, looking back, that I was living an unconscious life.

I had no idea thirty-four years ago about the power of choice. I simply allowed life to happen to me. Some of my unconscious choices led me into experiences of love while many offered life lessons the hard way. As I moved into the energy of my 30th year of life on earth I began to know that life as I knew it had to change. We make choices every day. Most of our choices are unconscious. Unconscious or not, every choice we make has the power to change our lives. A few of our choices are ones that will affect our lives for years, possibly even a lifetime.

I had been telling myself I would die by age thirty so I could endure the marriage I was in. I guess this was wishful thinking on my part, but at the time I didn't see any other way out of my life. Up until this stage of my life I didn't know I could have chosen a different experience any time I chose to do so. The closer I came to my thirties I realized I was not going to die. I knew I had to find the strength from within to change my life.

I didn't realize it at the time, but this was a major critical choice point in my life. Looking back, I realize now that the universe itself was redesigning itself to help me move through the new door that was opening. On December 31st, 1981 I knew I could no longer stay in my marriage. From deep within me came clear guidance along with *energy* that pushed me through the new door and onto a different path.

My marriage was over and I knew there was no turning back. At the time I felt a strength within me to change my entire life. I had no idea where this new found courage and *energy* was coming from but I trusted that I would find a way to rebuild my life.

On January 12th, 1981 I turned thirty. My marriage was over. I had two beautiful children; they were my reason for living. I had a 9th grade education and I had never worked outside the home. I was very wounded back then, unsure of myself. I did have faith in the power of God, but at that time in my life I was religious, meaning I followed the teachings of others, not what I knew in my heart to be true. I didn't question what I had been told by the elders. The first thirty years of my life, my initiations/experiences were trying to get me to step into my power. Without knowing it at the time ending my marriage was taking a step into embracing my power. By ending my marriage, I had chosen to step onto a different path.

Thirty years to learn one major life lesson may seem like a long time, but today I understand thirty years is a blink of an eye in the journey of the soul.

I was learning most of my life lessons the hard way. I call this "initiations through fire." I didn't know I had choices. I didn't know anything about the power of my thoughts and my emotions. I didn't know I was an incarnated soul. I didn't know anything about old outdated beliefs and how they influenced our lives. I didn't know that old outdated beliefs and patterns were the energy behind most of my choices. I have since learned that an old outdated belief is something we agreed to between the ages of birth and six years old. From these beliefs we accept certain things as true, which we then build our lives on.

My life, for the most part, was lived unconsciously. Up onto the thirtieth year of my life I was simply going through life like a robot. My tribe had taught me the language of man, not the language of soul. My tribe had taught me the laws of man, not the laws of the universe. My tribe taught me obedience. I was obedient to a fault.

The angels who once guided my life as a child were only memories pushed to the confines of my mind. Childhood imprinting and life experiences led me into making choices that created an unconscious life. I loved my children. They blessed my life in many wonderful ways. I was surrounded by family that loved me and the church was the center of my life but I was dying inside. I hid my pain from everyone. I knew how to shapeshift into someone else at the blink of an eye. This is true for many people; as children we learn the roles expected of us and we shapeshift into that role whenever needed.

Throughout my life I looked forward to going to sleep because of my dreams. Even though some of my dreams during my life were filled with nightmares, there were many more dreams filled with angels, peace and beautiful ethical places. I had no understanding during that time in my life that dreams are one way our soul and the world of spirit speak to us.

As I moved into my thirtieth year on earth my dreams began to change, they began guiding me. During this time in my life I was aware of being surrounded by light beings/ angels, but I didn't know how to call on them to guide me. The world of spirit had gotten me through the first thirty years of my life. I could feel the love of the angels; during the ages from ten to thirty I could not see them, but I could still feel them and God. The church and my parents never taught me that seeing angels was normal or that connection with God was something we all desired consciously or unconsciously. I had no concept of the soul except that my soul was something to be saved.

My husband and I had married very young. We were both children and we both had our wounds from childhood. Of course, those wounds surfaced and the marriage was not an easy one for either of us.

On New Year's Eve in 1981 I hit that critical choice point and there was no turning back. I knew I could no longer stay married. I needed to get out of the life I was living and since it looked like I was not going to die I knew I had to end my marriage. Looking back, I can see the initiations and experiences that led me into finally knowing I had to change my life.

I realize now that I was being guided by my soul. The *"energy"* that was guiding me to change my life had brought me to a crossroad.

Choosing to end my broken marriage was my pathway to liberating parts of self that were standing in the way of fully embracing the path of my soul. Of course I didn't understand any of this as it was all unfolding. I only knew that I my life was changing and I had to change with it.

For some reason I immediately focused all of my energy on getting a job; but I questioned doing what and would anyone hire someone who had no education. Someone at church mentioned a new nursing home that had just opened up. She said they were hiring.

That same night I had a dream about seeing a man in a long hallway. In my dream I was told to go to the nursing home and apply for a job. I had no idea back then but this was clear direction from my soul. In my dreams my soul opened up the path for me to go to that nursing home.

I had never worked outside my home, I had never driven more than ten miles from home, and I had not graduated from high school.

Was I scared? I don't remember feeling scared, but I was uncertain; however, I trusted that I would be taken care of. I trusted and had faith that all would be well. I didn't know it back then, but I was experiencing "Grace." I now understand that after we experience a series of initiations which lead us to a critical choice point once we have set foot on the new path the "Angel of Grace" enters into our lives. When Grace enters into our lives there is peace which surpasses all understanding despite the situation.

I remember driving to the nursing home to apply for the job. A very icy road was the path I had to travel to get to the nursing home. I remember telling myself as I sat in my car after my second attempt up the huge hill that I couldn't turn back.

I now understand that the long icy road was another initiation, one of many I would experience along my path as a modern day mystic. Everyone experiences initiations from the moment we are born.

Many of these experiences are not seen as initiations, but as challenges and roadblocks. In truth, these initiations open a pathway to liberate oneself from old outdated beliefs and patterns that block us from creating our experiences in love.

On that day thirty-four years ago that icy road was an initiation. How much did I want to change my life? What lengths would I go to step onto the path being illuminated by my soul? As I sat there at the bottom of the hill I could feel the same surge of *energy* I had felt the day I knew my marriage was over.

Something inside, some kind of *energy*, was pushing me to get up that hill. I knew if I could drive up that hill I could do anything. I took a deep breath and through tears I cried out for help. I asked my angels to help me drive the car up the hill. My car slipped all over the place, but I made it up the icy hill.

I applied for the job and was later told that anyone who would apply for a job in that kind of weather would be someone who showed up at work.

I was hired.

Key Points from this Chapter:

1. Everyone has a vibrational signature. This vibrational signature holds old outdated beliefs and patterns. Your personality's vibrational signature was created between birth and six years old based on the vibrational signatures of those around you. You create your experiences from your vibrational signature.

2. Everything we experience is formed from agreements we make. Nothing enters your life without you having first made an agreement to allow it to do so.

3. We arrive at a critical choice point after a series of initiations. Standing at this crossroad in our life we have a choice which path to take. The choice we make will determine the path one takes for learning soul lessons. I believe we each have six to eight major critical choice points in our lives.

4. Our soul will open the doors to a new path, but we must choose to go through the door.

5. Dreams are one way our soul communicates with each of us.

6. Many of the things we see as challenges and road-blocks, are actually initiations. Initiations open the doorway, a pathway, to liberate you from old outdated beliefs and patterns that block you from bringing forth your soul's dreams and visions.

7. Grace enters into our lives after we set foot on the new pathway.

8. As children, we learn the roles expected of us and we shapeshift into that role whenever needed.

Questions for reflection:

What are some of the initiations you have encountered along the journey?

Did you learn your life lessons through the initiations of Fire or Grace?

What are a few experiences that you now understand took you to critical choice points? (Experiences that brought your life to a crossroad where you had to choose which way to go.)

Do you remember a time in your life where you felt a push of energy guiding you to change your life? If so, did you move toward the change being asked of you or fight against it?

Looking back can you see a few "agreements" you made as a child that have shaped your life?

What roles did you shapeshift into as a child? Do you still shapeshift into these childhood roles today?

CHAPTER TWO

A Soul Connection

Looking back, I can clearly see that my soul and my angelic companions somehow helped me find my way onto a path that would change the rest of my life in amazing ways. Meeting John Guy Baublitz III was no accident; our souls orchestrated our meeting.

On January 20th, 1982 only twenty days after ending my marriage, I stepped onto a new path. I didn't know it at the time, but ending my marriage and making it up that icy hill led me to a new path, one I stepped onto with "Grace" by my side. Angel Grace does not make a grand announcement, but showers us with love and a sense of peace that surpasses all understanding. "Grace" is often experienced by the personality as feelings of strength and peace enter into our consciousness, even though we have just gone through a life changing experience. Despite the turmoil in my outer life and all of the uncertainty about my future, I felt a confidence that I had never experienced before in my life.

I understand now that ending my marriage and making it up the icy hill I had passed an initiation and was given the soul gifts of confidence, strength and Grace.

On the first day of my job I walked into the nursing home and looked around. Coming down the long hallway I saw a man in a wheelchair. My heart that had been so wounded and closed during my marriage skipped a beat when I looked at this stranger. I realized later that this was the hallway and the man I had seen in my dreams. I later found out his name, John Guy Baublitz III. I didn't know it at the time, but this man would change my life forever.

Looking back, I now understand there was INSTANT soul recognition when I saw Johnny. I also know, without a doubt, that Johnny and I met because it had been written. Our souls planned for us to meet during this lifetime. As I look back, I am still amazed at the timing of everything.

Here it was again - the path laid out my soul.

I didn't know anything about soul contracts or life plans, but I quickly realized I would move heaven and earth for John Guy Baublitz III. John was a resident at the nursing home. I found out later that he had moved into the nursing home two days before I began working there.

A few hours after starting work I was told to go to the shower room to help. You guessed it, Johnny was getting a shower. This was my formal introduction to him. The nurse's assistant who was giving Johnny a shower told me he was a zombie. She said he couldn't talk, nor walk and didn't seem to understand what was going on in the world around him. Due to a brain infection doctors had removed the left side of his brain and with it his skull. Many were repulsed by his physical appearance. They made him wear a huge piece of foam and a wig so he would look "normal."

Looking at Johnny, I once again felt this funny sensation inside of me. Thinking back, I know this was God recognizing Johnny. This was my soul silently letting me know that Johnny was someone I shared a soul contract with.

I quickly found out Johnny was anything but normal nor was he a zombie. He had simply shut out the world that had been so cruel to him, a world that did not see him. About a week later I was giving Johnny a shower and was talking to him like I did anyone. Suddenly he laughed. Tears come forth as I remember the moment I realized that Johnny understood what I was saying. I asked him, "Do you understand me?" He shook his head yes. Over the next few weeks and months I began to see patterns in Johnny's behavior. His bedroom was near to the door we entered when we signed in before starting work so every day I would stick my head in his room and say hello. He would smile and his eyes were bright and beautiful. About two hours later his eyes would be shut and he would be drooling. Long story short, we proved over time that Johnny had been living with a malfunctioning shunt in his brain. When he sat up the pressure caused him great pain and suffering. Everyone assumed he couldn't talk and walk because they had taken out his left brain several years earlier.

I am convinced that our souls brought us together. Many people believed I saved Johnny from a life doomed to live in silence and pain. The truth is we saved each other. This is the way our souls work; we meet the people we need to meet at actually the right time. There are no coincidences.

To make a long story short six months after meeting Johnny I moved him into my home. I knew that I could help him have a better life. I loved him. He almost felt like a part of me.

By this time I had proved that Johnny did understand EVERYTHING that was going on in the world around him.

I took him out of the nursing home which had refused to give him physical therapy. Everyone had given up on Johnny. He told me thirty years later that no one saw him back then, but somehow I saw him. Today I understand that the God in me saw the God in Johnny. Our souls knew each other. My two children and I taught him how to walk and talk. My parents helped me by making ramps and making our home handicapped accessible. I see now that we were all dedicated to Johnny. We each shared a soul contract with him. One that would touch our lives during the next thirty years in powerful ways.

I married Johnny a year later and I spent the next thirty years of his life making sure he was safe from a world that did not SEE him. I have no doubt that our souls orchestrated our meeting each other, for it had been written as a part of our soul's life plan.

Through the next thirty years Johnny would become one of my greatest teachers. His greatest gift was unconditional love and his ability to see the glass half full at all times. I once asked him if he ever questioned why this all happened to him and he said, "No, why not me."

He taught me more about faith, love and God than any religion could have taught me.

I didn't question my love and commitment to Johnny. I knew wherever my journey took me, I would keep him safe.

Bringing Johnny home was another critical choice point in my life. I had come to another crossroads and the path I chose was the path that included Johnny. This one choice would be the foundation for the next thirty years of my life.

I remind you that a critical choice point is a time in one's life when we come to a crossroad. The choice we make will determine the path one takes for learning soul lessons. I believe we each have six or eight major critical choice points in our lives. Within six months I had experienced two crossroads, each leading me to the next one.

During the next eight years life revolved around Johnny. I realized many years later that I put all my time and attention into taking care of Johnny. I didn't take time to heal from my childhood wounds and my marriage.

I became Johnny's advocate. I became confident because I had to fight the medical community that had given up on

Johnny. I was his voice and his advocate and no one was going to hurt Johnny. Because I had to be an advocate for Johnny I learned how to stand up to authority. This was another major gift that Johnny gave me. I can laugh now, but during our thirty years together I kicked more than one doctor or nurse out of his hospital room. Because of Johnny I learned to use my voice and I learned that I was much more powerful than I knew I was.

My life with Johnny was a good life, but I didn't have very good boundaries. I continued to make choices that I can now see were not in alignment with my soul's life plan. These choices continued to create some very difficult life lessons for me.

I loved Johnny with all that I was, however, there was still something missing in my life. I had shut down so many parts of myself during the first thirty years of my life. As I grew in confidence I also began wanting more in my life. Johnny was happy. He could walk and talk. He was surrounded by a tribe that loved him and was devoted to him. I borrowed money and bought him a computer. This opened his life in new ways and he now had an outlet to express himself creatively. He was now able to communicate in different ways. He would spend eight hours a day with his computer.

John was happy, but, having focused all my energy on Johnny, once he was happy and stable medically I had a lot of left over energy.

I still didn't know who I was. There was a void in me, a huge void. I was still living an unconscious life. During this time I continued to talk to God. I would go out at night and look at the stars and cry. I went to church, but somehow I knew my answers were not going to be found there. What was I searching for? I had no clue. I only knew there was a restlessness within me.

In 1987 I received what I call a major soul boot. Today I know it was a soul realignment. A soul realignment comes via many different life experiences; for me it was a nervous breakdown. Memories from my childhood flooded my consciousness and I could no longer smile or laugh my way through the floodgates of emotions that I had stored away in the confines of my mind.

I was quickly sent away to a rehab, which was the popular thing to do in the 80's. Leaving Johnny was one of the hardest things I had to do, but I knew my family would take care of him.

Looking back, I can clearly see this was a soul realignment. Soul realignments happen when one's soul determines that the personality has strayed so far from the soul's life-plan that something needs to happen to help the personality STOP and reevaluate one's life.

Soul realignments usually occur as a health crisis, or a major life change.

For me it was a nervous breakdown. Being sent away from home would be the catalyst that began making me question what I had been taught by my tribe.

Up until this point in my life I had been very secluded and didn't question much of anything. During my time away from the tribe I began finding a new me. I didn't know it at the time, but the nervous breakdown occurred so I could begin to move my life away from the beliefs of my tribe to embracing the guidance of my soul.

This was a major transitional point in my life. In an unconscious world a nervous breakdown or a disease/health condition is experienced as a destructive force in one's life. In truth the experience has entered our life because "someone" is watching over each one of us and that "someone" is helping us move our life back into alignment with the plan of our soul.

While at the rehab I experienced a shift of consciousness and there was no turning back. I was waking up and beginning to align my life with my soul's life plan. As I began releasing old outdated beliefs of my tribe my vibrational signature began changing.

Interesting enough many years later I realized that this great shift in my life occurred during what is known as the convergence years.

The convergence occurred between 1987 and 2012. During these years many people like myself would experience a soul realignment. These soul realignments opened doorways for growth and expansion should the personality choose to go through the door. Life as one knows it changes.

As I have mentioned before, we all go through many initiations during our lives. Life itself is a series of initiations. Many of these experiences and events in our lives go by unnoticed because we haven't been taught that we are incarnated souls. We haven't been taught that many of these experiences which we see as destroying our lives are really experiences that are meant to help us STOP and reevaluate our life.

Recognizing the signs of spirit that guide us becomes the quest of the modern day mystic. The modern day mystic opens up to seeing EVERYTHING in our lives as having a divine purpose.

For me it was a nervous breakdown that was the STOP sign. This was a transitional point in my life. During transitional points in our lives the initiations/experiences focus on helping the personality move from a path that is not in alignment with the soul's dream to a crossroad. At every crossroad there are usually two or three pathways to choose from. All paths lead to new experiences for soul growth and soul expansion. There is never a wrong path, for every path, every step, we take leads the modern day mystic to knowing God through every experience.

Key Points:

1. We recognize those we share soul contracts with via our soul's vibrational signature.

2. There is a plan created for us by our soul.

3. Soul realignments happen when one's soul determines that the personality has strayed so far from the soul's life-plan that something needs to

happen to help the personality STOP and reevaluate one's life. A soul realignment comes via many different life lessons.

4.   "Grace" is often experienced by the personality as feelings of strength and peace enter into our consciousness, even though we have just gone through a life changing experience.

5.   Everything in our lives has a Divine Purpose.

Questions for reflection:

What are a few initiations/experiences that you now understand took you to a critical choice point? (Experiences that brought your life to a crossroad where you had to choose the next pathway to take.)

As you stood at the crossroads did you see the different paths you could take?

Looking back can you see different times in your life where you came to a crossroad and chose to stay on the same path? (We do this because we are comfortable in the life we are living even though we are not happy.)

Looking back in your life can you see when you experienced a soul realignment? (Stop and reevaluate your life)

Have you ever felt "Grace" in your life during times of uncertainty and change? (To me Grace is experienced as calm in the middle of a storm.)

Have you ever met someone and felt that sense of knowing them?

Can you recognize the times in your life when your soul was guiding you? If so list a few.

CHAPTER THREE

Dark Night of the Soul

When I returned home after thirty days in rehab I was truly not the same person. My confidence had been building since I met Johnny, but now I had a pair of new eyes in which I saw the world and my life. Now I wanted to know who I was and I why was I here. The church which used to be my refuge became a place to which I no longer felt I belonged.

About six months after my soul realignment I stopped going to church. This had been my community since I was born. I was sad but knew I would not find my answers inside the church. During this time my relationship with Jesus also took on new meaning. My Jesus was not here to save me but to guide me. I loved Jesus with all that I was and realized no one could take that love away. During this time my dreams began to guide me once again. My angelic companions began coming into my waking consciousness. It was a time of spiritual and emotional growth for me.

Coming out of rehab I began seeing a therapist. Once again, I can see how my soul guided me to "Karen." She saw herself as a therapist, but I saw her as my healer, my teacher and guide. Once the floodgates opened up I was on the path of healing my childhood wounds. As I let go of the past I continued to experience initiations. Some of my major life lessons were still learned through Fire (the hard way) and others were learned through Grace. I also went back to school. I wanted to become a therapist so that I could help others.

At times I felt overwhelmed with all of the life changes. I realize, looking back, I was still shapeshifting through my life. By this I meant very few people knew that I was feeling overwhelmed. I had learned as a child to smile despite what I was really feeling. I was very good at figuring out what role someone wanted me to play. Of course I had no idea how much energy this took and that I was not being authentic. It was about two years after my Soul Realignment when I experienced another major initiation.

It was during this time period that I experienced what many people call the dark night of the soul. I define the dark night of the soul at a time in the personality's life when they feel a sense of overwhelming disconnection from everything and everyone, including is feeling the love of the world of spirit and God. The personality becomes so overwhelmed with emotions and feelings they get pulled into the rabbit hole of despair and the shadow energy temporarily blocks one from experiencing the light of one's soul.

Our soul does not experience what we call the dark night of the soul; however, the **personality** feels a sense of overwhelming disconnection from everything and everyone including feeling the love of the world of spirit.

The dark night of the soul is a time in the life of the modern day mystic when they go through the initiations of illumination and purification.

At some point during the time of disconnection the personality cries out for help and this opens the doorway for the world of spirit to enter in and in doing so begins a transformational experience like none other. The personality receives a soul infusion of energy that burns away core old outdated limiting beliefs about oneself and the world. This initiation becomes a transitional point in one's life and the journey becomes one of shedding of the old self so the new self can be reborn. Of course I didn't have this information while I was going through my own dark night of my soul.

This was a time of great confusion, separation, and despair in my life. Even me ending my marriage and my nervous breakdown did not compare to what I was now experiencing. Dying was preferred by me.

This is the first time in my life I questioned God.

I remember lying in my bed crying out to God to please take me "home." I couldn't see through the despair and feelings that flooded my consciousness. I felt disconnected from my tribe and other people. It was a time of disorientation and disconnection from what I had always believed about God. By now I understood that God wasn't a "he" but was energy. I knew that God still heard me and I knew I was a part of God, but for the first time in my life I felt alone, abandoned even by God. When this despair and anguished came over me, I was unprepared for the disconnection from God I was experiencing. Even during the wounding from childhood experiences and my first marriage, I knew that God was with me.

Suddenly this void entered into my consciousness and I felt alone and lost.

This lasted for months.

During the day I would go through the motions, shapeshifting my way through life, but at night, in the refuge of my bedroom, I would plead for help. I would mostly plead for God to take me home. I didn't like it here and I didn't think I could finish doing what I had been sent here to do. It was during one of these experiences where I was begging to go home to God and pleading for help that my bedroom was suddenly filled with angels and light.

The light was all consuming.

I felt like I was taken out of my body. I don't remember how long I was out of my body, but when I came back into my body I was different. Every cell of my being had been changed by the light.

I was renewed and I began seeing the world and everything that had occurred in my life up to that point as being in Divine Order. Nothing, and I do mean nothing had the power it once did. Old outdated beliefs were released and the rabbit hole of despair was never to be an option again. I now understand that everyone's experience through the initiations of illumination and purification is different. Many people experience this transformation gradually and many experience the transformation while they are sleeping.

Looking back, I would compare the dark night of the soul as a near death experience (NDE). After a NDE the personality has been forever changed and experiences life via the lens of new eyes and new consciousness. For me the new eyes and new consciousness were spiritual consciousness. This simply means that everything in one's life is viewed from the lens of spiritual consciousness versus physical consciousness.

Physical consciousness has the personality focus on the physical experiences via the physical senses. Spiritual consciousness enhances the physical senses and brings forth intuition to the forefront. Intuition is clear guidance from soul.

As children our intuition is schooled and parented out of us. As children, we are taught to follow the rules and not to use our imagination. We are taught to conform. We are taught to color in the lines and listen to everyone in the outer world.

Intuition, soul guidance, is pushed aside for what we can hear, taste, touch, smell and see.

Because we are not taught that we are incarnated souls, we don't see the initiations of our lives. Therefore, when we enter into an initiation like the dark night of the soul we think we are going crazy. The dark night of the soul is not seen as an initiation, but as deep depression. Doctors unschooled in the ways of the soul do not know how to "treat" this initiation and offer medications and other procedures that actually stop the experience. Intervention by the medical community untrained in the ways of the soul actually blocks the fires of illumination and purification from burning away the aspects of self that are not in alignment with love.

This is a hindrance and many personalities never move through the initiations of illumination and purification. They will continue to feel this deep depression, despair, no matter how much the doctor tries to medicate it away, until the initiations of illumination and purification have been successfully completed. I am not advising people not to take their medications that are prescribed by their doctors. I am simply saying that if we understood that we are spiritual beings, perhaps care of the spiritual aspect of who we are would help people move through these initiations.

The fires of illumination and purification and the dark night of the soul are a precursor to self-realization. Before this self-realization can occur Grace and connection to God are temporarily blocked out as is the light so one can move to the place of self-realization.

When we understand that the dark night of the soul is a blessing in the life of the modern day mystic, perhaps we will move into the initiation with a new understanding. The fires of illumination and purification burn away the imprints and beliefs that pull the personality away from love.

After the dark night of the soul one begins to see through the lens of spiritual consciousness. The modern day mystic knows at their core that there is only love and everything else is an illusion. There is no fear of separation because the modern day mystic understands at the core of their being that their heart is God's heart and their experiences are God's experience. There is no separation and there is nothing one has to do but open up and allow God to be experienced in one's life.

The gift of the dark night of the soul is self-realization.

Although the dark night of the soul is something everyone must go through alone, perhaps knowing that many have gone through the dark night of the soul will help. Perhaps knowing that the initiation experienced during the dark night of the soul is actually the fires of illumination and purification will help the modern day mystic find new ways to move through this time. Perhaps knowing that ages ago all mystics went through the dark night of the soul and the fire of illumination and purification, but did so while safely secluded and watched over by their spiritual teacher will help the modern day mystic implement measures that will help them move though this initiation. Turning to a spiritual teacher schooled in the ways of the soul can help to reassure you that you are not crazy and you will move from this place of darkness and when you do you will literally be reborn.

Key Points:

1. The dark night of the soul is a time in the personality's life when they feel a sense of overwhelming disconnection from everything and everyone including feeling the love of the world of spirit, of God.

2. During the dark night of the soul the modern day mystic goes through the initiations of illumination and purification.

3. The dark night of the soul is actually a blessing because the personality has arrived at a transitional point in life which can lead to self-realization.

4. After moving through the initiations of illumination and purification the modern day mystic knows there is only love and everything is an illusion.

5. When going through the dark night of the soul one should turn to a spiritual teacher for help.

Questions for reflection:

Have you experienced a dark night of the soul?

Understanding that the dark night of the soul is a blessing in the life of the modern day mystic what would you do different?

How has your life changed after you moved through the initiations of illumination and purification?

Once again, I have mentioned how I shaped shifted through this experience. Can you see how the shape-shifter has entered your life?

CHAPTER FOUR

Seeing Life Through the Lens of Spiritual Consciousness

Slowly, over the next two years I began SEEING with a new site. As a little girl I could SEE, but by the age of about ten I had been humanized and the world of spirit was pushed to the confines of my mind; this is true for most children. Now angels became my guides and my constant companions. It was as if angels were lighting a path and all I had to do was follow it. I realize this sounds over-simplified, but after the initiations of illumination and purification everything in my life was seen via the lens of spiritual consciousness. My intuitive mind began to guide me. Of course I didn't see the connectedness of everything back then. I continued feeling the *energy* that was guiding me. I still wasn't sure what this *energy* was but I knew when I followed it the path before me became clearer.

I was now forty-four years old and a senior in college. I was interning at the local AIDS Hospice. It had been two years since I experienced the dark night of my soul, six years since my soul realignment and thirteen years after I met Johnny. The experiences at the hospice opened me up to new experiences and new gifts. My gifts of sight and touch began to awaken within me. I could see what many of the nurses around me could not see -angels, spirit guides, and those who had birthed into spirit. Since that day on the icy road, fourteen years earlier, my confidence, spiritual sight, and connection to the world of spirit had grown and expanded. God was being experienced in every experience.

The hospice and the people I met there who had AIDS were major teachers during this time. Looking back, I know I met several people with whom I shared soul contracts. I found my voice as an advocate once again. As I once advocated for Johnny I now advocated for many of the patients in regards to what they were experiencing. I began educating the nurses to stop denying those who were birthing into spirit their reality. I knew the patients were seeing with different eyes than the nurses and their families and I knew I was seeing with different eyes also.

I was awakening. Seeing life through the lens of spiritual consciousness gave everything a new focus.

With the awakening I had experienced after my dark night of my soul my gifts of sight continued to open in new and amazing ways. This was a magical time in my life. I was still going through initiations on fire, but now I moved quickly through the life lessons. I was experiencing enchantment in my life once again as I did many years earlier in my grandmother's garden. Hearing God through nature and the wind was experienced by me as they had been when I was a child. The world was alive with the sound of God and so was my life.

My angelic companions became my teachers. I began remembering where I was "traveling" to during my dreams. During this time I would wake up knowing I had been with my spiritual teachers during my dreams but didn't share them with anyone. There were still wounded parts of myself that wanted to fit in. I can laugh about it now because it is impossible to fit in when we are each born to stand out. We use so much energy trying to fit in, that we box ourselves in and live very small lives.

As I grew spiritually it became impossible to fit in the box. My consciousness was expanding and so was my life. I could feel myself being guided by the world of spirit; however, I still had to get up every day and live the life that I had created and most of it was based on old outdated beliefs and patterns and childhood wounding.

Although my spiritual life was expanding, my personal life was a mess. I was still trying to please everyone. This pleasing everyone had become a pattern of life. I had learned at a very early age that if I made people happy I would be safe. Unfortunately, making everyone else happy had its cost.

The cost was that I still didn't know who I was. I was still trying to please everyone around me. I was being guided to change my life, but the old outdated beliefs and patterns were still, for the most part, running my life. This was a good time in my life, but it was also a time of confusion. A core belief I had was that you take care of everyone else first. You put their needs and making them happy before your own. Some part of me knew putting myself first was a loving thing to do, but the old outdated beliefs continued to make me feel guilty every time I made a choice that I knew was right for me but would greatly affect someone I loved. I have since learned that when I make a choice that is in alignment with love for myself, it is the right choice for everyone. I have also learned that my life was being influenced by archetypal energy known as the prostitute energy.

Archetypal energies are constantly influencing our behaviors. Archetypal patterns affect every aspect of your life. During this time in my life I had no understanding of archetypal energies and how one's soul will use these energies to help us move through initiations and life lessons. They were guiding me none the less and were greatly influencing my life.

I have since learned the language of archetypes because this is one key way our soul communicates with us.

Although my spiritual life was expanding, my personal life was a mess. That said, life was good because I now understood that life was a mystical journey.

My life with Johnny began to change as I began to move through consciousness shifts. I understood that I loved him, but our relationship was not based on physical love; instead, it was soul love. He was my soul mate and I knew I would cover him and take care of him.

Truth is Johnny was the heart of our family. We called him Johnny angel. His wisdom touched many lives and his humor was a gift to anyone who knew him.

Everyone who met Johnny loved him. Everyone who met him believed he was an angel in human form. I know he was an angel in my life and I honor him to this day as one of my major teachers. I believe during our lives we meet many "angels" who bring us a special message and life lessons. These messages and life lessons can impact our lives in major ways.

As I grew and evolved my personal relationships took many forms. I had two intimate relationships with women. Both of these relationships taught me major life lessons, mainly through the initiations of fire. I will always be grateful for the experience of loving them. I realize now that when we shift our lives spiritually there can be a huge separation between one's spiritual awareness and one's life. Merging one's spiritual life and one's physical life together is the quest for the modern day mystic.

I continued healing my childhood wounds and growing spiritually. Life was good. As I continued to grow and evolve my journey took a major turn and I discovered Reiki.

Key Points:

1. Seeing life through the lens of spiritual consciousness gives everything a new focus.

2. Merging one's spiritual life and one's physical life together is the quest for the modern day mystic.

3. As we grow spiritually the initiations through fire are moved through quickly and with less resistance.

4. During our lives, we meet many "angels" who bring us special messages and life lessons. These messages and life lessons can impact our lives in major ways.

5. Intuition is guidance from the soul.

6. Archetypal energies are constantly influencing our behaviors. Archetypal patterns affect every aspect of your life.

Questions for Reflection:

Do you see and experience life via physical consciousness or spiritual consciousness?

Looking back can you see a few of the earth angels and the message and /or life lesson they had for you?

Have you learned to listen and follow your intuition? (Intuition is guidance from your soul. It can be experienced as a gut hunch, a thought in your head, a dream)

Are you learning your lessons through the initiations of Fire or Grace? (Initiations by Fire is the hard way. Although the experience might be a difficult one when experienced through Grace there is a sense of understanding and peace as one moves through the experience.)

Do you feel guilty when you put yourself first?

In what ways do you experience the energy of prostitute? I remind you that the energy of prostitute comes into our lives when we negate the power of our soul for anything, be it, love, money, approval, safety, etc.

CHAPTER FIVE

The Teacher Reiki

I will always remember when I first met Reiki, in this lifetime. I had gone to a class that promoted a way to heal the wounded parts of self. The teachers had us lay on the floor and guided us through breath work. As I moved into a trance like state they began drumming. I'm not sure what all occurred, but suddenly the teachers placed their hands on me. One woman put her hands on my heart, and the other woman put her hands on my feet. I heard one of them say to let go. I remember tears falling from my eyes because I was feeling an expanded state of consciousness. I felt immersed in love. I began to travel. I left my body and was taken to the world of spirit.

It was amazing.

I wasn't sleeping, but I also knew I wasn't in my body. I began feeling a warm energy coming from their hands. This warm energy seemed to spread throughout my entire body. As the energy moved around it seemed to be healing me. I told myself, when I could talk, I would ask the teachers about the energy.

When I found my voice I asked the teachers what had just happened. They smiled and said, "Reiki."

In that moment I found Reiki. Reiki became another major teacher that would lead me into bringing forth more of my soul's dreams and visions.

Another major choice point came about six months later when I chose to become attuned to Reiki. I had talked myself out of going to the Reiki class, but my partner convinced me to go. Putting myself first and wanting something for me was still difficult for me. My partner drove me to the class that was two hours away. She believed in me. Thinking back, I wonder how her life would have turned out if she had taken the Reiki class with me instead of sitting in the car. I realize now that the initiation of Reiki changed everything in my life, including my relationship with my partner.

Being attuned to Reiki opened me up energetically. Reiki began teaching me and I began doing energy healing sessions. My intuitive gifts opened up and I began to grow in confidence with sharing the messages from the world of spirit.

I began teaching Reiki and had a wonderful practice helping my clients heal. I was known as the Reiki lady and the angel lady. Everyone knew about my love of Reiki and my love of the angels.

During this time I also learned that I had energy anatomy and I learned about chakras. I quickly began teaching about the path of the chakras. It was as if just hearing the word chakra opened my consciousness to higher learning from my guides. Each chakra has a different life lesson and gift to learn. I realize now that the chakras, each offer an initiation. I also understand now that the initiations of illumination and purification also cleanse the chakras. It was around this time that I began to understand that we are vibrational beings and everything that we see is in a constant state of motion, including our lives.

I began walking my spiritual path in earnest; my life had to fit into my spiritual path. Most people try to fit their spiritual path into their physical lives, but for me it was the other way around. My spiritual path was my life. As a modern day mystic God was now the core of every experience.

My dreams began teaching me what I was to teach to my students. I would wake up inspired to create a new class. I was being guided by my dreams, but I still had no conscious understanding about soul and soul life. I continued talking to God, but now my experience of God expanded once again. It is hard to describe how one can experience God even more deeply than I did after my deep night of the soul initiation, but I found that every day I was learning something new about love, and about myself.

I will forever be grateful for my religious upbringing because through it I grew to love and know Jesus. As I grew and evolved I began to understand my Jesus was very different than what the church had taught me about Jesus. My Jesus did not save me because he died on a cross. My Jesus guided me how to live a life of love right now, right here, on earth. He taught me to love. He taught me to embrace my truth and to bring forth the Christ within me so that I too might be like Jesus, right now, right here on earth - a being of love.

Around this time I made a decision to learn my life lessons via love. Jesus, and my angels were my guides. Jesus continues to be a guiding force in my life today. Although I had stopped going to church many years earlier, I still struggled with where Jesus fit into my life. I slowly realized I was now spiritual but not religious. My religion had taught me to put Jesus and myself in a box. I now knew Jesus didn't have to "fit" into anything, nor did I. I was beginning to understand what it meant to be the creative force in my life, but I still didn't understand the power of choice and my thoughts. Today, as a teacher of soul I teach my students that they are the creative force in their life. This simply means that through their thoughts and emotions they create their experiences.

I slowly began to understand that being spiritual was my way of "being" in the world and being religious had been my way of "seeing" the world.

Living a spiritual life simply means experiencing God through every activity and experience. The modern day mystic sees the world through the eyes of God, which see only love. There is no dogma to follow for love is the only instruction, we are given by God. Be only love, know only love through every experience, personality and activity; this is the quest for the modern day mystic as he/she embraces being a spiritual being.

My Christian faith which once guided me no longer was my focus. I no longer saw the world through the lens of my religion.

I struggled with this for many years because I thought if I didn't embrace being a Christian I was somehow denying Jesus and his teachings. It took me twenty years, but today I understand Jesus was a mystic and was spiritual. His way of being in the world was love. I'm not so sure that Jesus would be thrilled at what people do in his name.

As I practiced Reiki my intuitive gifts continued to expand. Seeing angels became my new norm. Being guided by them was as natural as breathing. During this time I remember getting an intuitive reading from a woman. She told me I was guided by my soul and that I didn't need her or anyone else to give me messages from spirit.

At this time I didn't really know what she meant. I had no conscious understanding about soul other than what I had learned from the church. I only knew I loved God with all that I was and that my relationship with God was the relationship I wanted to deepen.

Life was good. My two children had grown into amazing adults. I was a grandma. Johnny continued to be happy despite the many changes in my life. I was teaching classes about chakras, angels, Reiki and more.

At this time my relationship with God and the world of spirit began to be all consuming, but I still had to live in the "real" world. I also began being more authentic. By this I mean I began using the shape-shifter in ways that empowered my life. I also began allowing people to see me, the real me. This meant allowing people to know that I wasn't always happy. I learned I had a whole range of emotions and feelings and I didn't need to hide them by shapeshifting into someone else.

As I continued to grow and evolve my dream life took me into new dimensions and I found myself dreaming about a man. These dreams really shook me to the core. I was in a relationship with a woman and had no conscious thoughts about being with a man. However, my dreams were guiding me to wanting to experience the love of a man. Not just any man, but a man who I wanted to know in deeper, physical ways. By this time I knew to trust my dreams, even when I was confused by them.

Today I understand my dreams were how my soul was guiding me.

Key Points:

1. We are vibrational beings and everything that we see is in a constant state of motion, including our lives.

2. We have energy anatomy which includes chakras.

3. Each chakra offers an initiation.

4. Being spiritual is a way of "being" in the world, being religious is a way of "seeing" the world.

5. Dreams are one way your soul communicates with you.

Reflections:

Would you describe yourself as spiritual or religious?

Are you aware of any dreams that have guided your life?

Have you ever experienced a spontaneous healing be it spiritual, physical or emotional?

Do you experience having any spiritual guides/angels in your life?

CHAPTER SIX

Dreaming in the Dreams of My Soul

My dreams became to intensify and I began to be downloaded with spiritual information. At the same time my dreams also intensified about loving a man. Not just any man, but someone I already knew. He was already in my life as a teacher and a friend, but consciously I had no thoughts about him being anything more in my life. He was married. I was in a committed relationship and even though we had grown apart, I had no conscious desire to be with anyone.

My dreams and my soul had other plans. I know this is hard for many personalities to understand, but when our souls want something they will use whatever means they can to wake us up.

This includes shaking up our lives. To say my life was shaken up when I began dreaming of a man would be an understatement.

I now know that our dreams are one way our souls communicate with us. During this time my dreams once again took on new meaning. I began seeing in new ways. My gifts of sight began surfacing even when I wasn't working with a client on my healing table. I began waking up every day writing about things I saw in my dreams.

Amazingly, the information from the world of spirit began to flood into my consciousness. I believe Reiki opened me up during this time to experiencing higher states of consciousness. I was giving Reiki sessions everyday, but I was also receiving Reiki sessions and because of this I began releasing old outdated beliefs.

The distance between my partner and I grew. It seemed that as I grew spiritually, I emotionally moved more away from her. I realize now that our vibrational signatures were no longer compatible.

I couldn't share my dreams with her. I did tell my best friend Shirl about my dreams and wanting to be with a man, she said, "Maybe the feelings will go away."

The feelings didn't go away, they only intensified. I began experiencing this "push of energy" to wanting to experience the love of the man in my dreams.

I had been sixteen when I married my first husband. We were both young and didn't know how to love ourselves much less someone else. The love I continued to feel for Johnny was pure and was based on soul love. I was committed to keeping him safe and loved him to the core of my being, but I had not experienced this kind of connection in any relationship. I needed guidance and went to an event and was guided to get an angel reading.

I didn't know it at the time, but I was still looking for someone else to guide me instead of trusting my own intuition and guidance. The angel woman laughed and asked why I was there. She reminded me I was connected and receiving spiritual guidance. She said, "You know you are not a lesbian. There is a man that wants to love you and you already know him." I was shaken by her words. How could she know about my dreams? I knew what she said was true. Hearing her confirm what I already knew because of my dreams I went home and called my teacher, my friend. He confirmed that he too was having dreams and that yes, we needed to talk. He said, "I knew you were going to be with a man and the man was him." I can remember the feelings that flooded my body. I was scared, excited, still in a state of disbelief, but trusting that whatever was happening was in alignment with some grand plan.

I turned my partner's life upside down because I ended our relationship based on what I was feeling from my dreams. How could she understand when I myself didn't? She was very angry and began to lash out at me. This time in my life was bittersweet, because I hurt her. At the same time I had to follow my heart and my heart now wanted to experience the love of a man.

My relationship with "Edward" was all consuming and through him I began experiencing a physical union with a man. Despite the fact that he was married and I had ended my relationship with my partner, my relationship with God and the world of spirit intensified during this time.

It's hard to explain, but my relationship with Edward was opening me up to knowing union with God in deeper ways.

Fifteen years later I now know that what I was experiencing were mystical experiences. My love of God deepened as my heart opened up into loving "Edward." The universe was using Edward to help me heal.

We became lovers in the spring. Parts of me that I didn't even know existed began to emerge. Parts that I had suppressed because of childhood wounds began to spring forth for healing and transformation.

During the month of May I went on a spiritual retreat. Five days of silence. My spiritual director told me no books, and no giving sessions. This was my time to be with Jesus. The silence at first was frightening, but quickly I allowed my body and my mind to attune to being in the silence and being with God in a deeper way. The only time we could talk was the hour with our spiritual director once a day.

During one of the sessions my spiritual director had me close my eyes. He was reading something from the Bible and suddenly I felt a fire in my heart chakra. It burnt and physically hurt. I opened my eyes and asked what had just happened? He said he didn't know but had seen a flame jump out of my heart. He later talked to a priest and the priest told him what had occurred, but to be honest I forget. I only know that the fire that arose from my heart was another turning point in my life both physically and spiritually. I was forever changed. My spirit teachers later told me the Flame of Christ had been ignited within me. I now understand that this was a spiritual activation.

During June and July the time spent with Edward was all consuming and seemed to bring me into deeper communion with God. I began writing about spiritual keys and bringing forth higher teachings of light during this time. I didn't really know what any of it meant, but trusted that I would understand the information when the time was right.

Again, I did not understand soul contracts and soul agreements during this time. I now understand that our souls used our soul love, which never ends, to awaken us both from living lives that were not in alignment with our soul's life plan.

By the end of July my dreams that had guided me toward Edward were now beginning to pull me away from him.

How could this be, I asked God, the angels, and my soul?

Why would you bring this love into my life to take it away?

I was confused, but knew I had to end our lover connection.

I loved Edward with every part of my being. When we began our love affair I didn't think about where it would lead us. I only knew that we had been led to one another. The same energy that had pulled me toward Edward was now pulling me away from him. I had also been shown in a dream that if Edward and I continued our love affair we would be taken on a path of learning by fire. I'm sure my soul showed me this to help me find the courage to end our lover relationship. My life had already changed because I ended my relationship with my partner. Edward was beginning to feel the guilt of being with me and not being ready to end his marriage.

I had learned to follow my inner guidance I received from my dreams. Edward always took off the month of August so I knew we would have no contact. During this time I prayed for Edward to come to his senses and know also that our lover connection had to end. Sure enough, when he returned home, he ended our lover connection. We both knew it was the right thing to do. We both felt the sting and heartache. I had learned to trust my dreams so I trusted that although I did not understand, God would reveal all in time.

Thinking back, I can clearly see that there was a window of opportunity that allowed our soul love to intervene and help set us on a path that could be used to move us from the lives that we had created. Edward's marriage needed to end, but not because of me. I knew that Edward needed to walk that walk without me. His soul simply used me to awaken him to parts of self that he had kept buried. My soul used my soul love for Edward to awaken me and to learn how to allow a man to love me.

I knew I would love "Edward" forever, but I knew we had to go our separate paths. The window of opportunity that had opened because of our soul love was now closing. We are so used to living by the rules of our tribe and what we are told are the social norms that most people think a love affair is morally wrong. I now understand that soul love can and will be used to awaken and heal parts of self that need to be healed. By ending our love affair we were able to walk away with the gifts of our union. Had we stayed the course I have no doubt it would have been a very different ending.

Edward was not available to love me completely. At the time it felt like parts of me were being torn apart, but I trusted that it was the right thing to do. I believed Edward's marriage needed to end, but not because of me. I knew that Edward needed to walk that walk without me. I knew that Edward had to find his way without me.

We had both arrived at a crossroad and this time the choice we each made was to go onto a different path. One that would lead our lives into very different initiations and experiences.

As I think back my heart still jumps at the thought of Edward; he has been such a strong force in my life. He opened my heart up and my very being to wanting to be loved by a man. Through him I experienced an awakening, one that would shape the rest of my life. We didn't stay in physical contact during the years that have passed; however, Edward was only a dream a way. Throughout the past fifteen years I would feel a tug on my heart and I knew Edward was going through his own initiations. I could tell many of them were by fire. At times I visited him in my dreams.

As I grew in understanding the ways of the soul, I began to understand that Edward and I shared a soul contract. Soul contracts are sacred and binding contracts entered into with love between souls. I also believe that Edward is my twin flame. A twin flame is another soul that was cast from the core of God at the same time. Twin flames may or may not meet during any given life, but when they do, the experience is one that is deeply transforming. Even though the timing of our connection was not the best I believe today that Edward was used to heal me in ways that only a twin flame can do. I also know that I awakened parts of Edward that he didn't know existed. I have no doubt that he was changed by our connection as deeply as I was; he had experienced an awakening within himself.

As the years have passed there have been many times I wanted to reach out to Edward but was guided not to do so. In my heart, I believed, and I still believe that our paths would intersect again one day. Although our souls had guided us to each other and the experience was one that would be forever etched upon my heart, I know without any doubt that at the time, going on different paths was the only choice. Had we chosen to continue our love affair we would have gone through the fires of initiation together and this would not have been in anyone's highest good.

At the time choosing a different path was the hardest thing I've ever had to do because our love was beyond anything I had ever experienced. That said, at the core of my being I knew I had to travel a different path. Once again, I had arrived at a crossroad in my life. I also knew I needed to find a man who could and would love me completely.

During this time my dreams and my life once again took on new meaning.

I began to understand that my soul was not something to be saved but was actively guiding me via my dreams. My connection with my soul deepened. In the fall of 2000 I began a quest to find my spiritual mate. I knew via my dreams I would meet a man and we would teach together the things I was learning via my dreams. He would be a spiritual man and would be available to love me.

I began to teach my students what I was learning about the soul. I also began doing "research" to find my next life partner. This journey of research led me into many great adventures. The men I met taught me a lot about myself. It was clear I still had a very wounded little girl self-image and I found myself giving my heart away to men who didn't want it or knew what a precious gift it was.

Around this time Angel Ariel came into my life. Archangel Ariel entered my consciousness during a session I received from my friend Deb in 1999.

Keys Points:

1. We are downloaded with information and guidance from our soul during our dreams.

2. When our soul wants to move our lives in a different direction it will use whatever means possible to get our attention.

3. Soul contracts are sacred and binding contracts entered into with love between souls.

4. Twin flames are cast from the core of God at the same time.

5. Physical union with another can open us up to deeper connection with God.

6. We would be wise to trust the guidance of soul.

Questions for Reflection:

Have you ever been guided by a dream to change your life and doing so changed the lives of people you loved?

Have you ever received clear guidance via your dreams or intuition to do something that you didn't understand at the time?

If you do receive such guidance do you trust it enough to follow it even when it doesn't make sense at the time?

Have you experienced a relationship that did not conform to the conventional rules and norms regarding relationships?

Have you ever experienced God through a sexual connection?

Looking at your life can see you any soul contracts that helped you heal parts of self even though the timing wasn't the greatest?

CHAPTER SEVEN

Activations and Light Body Changes

A ngel Ariel was new to me and they told me they came to help me heal my heart. During this time I continued to release emotions from my childhood experiences; I cried, and cried and cried. I cried for my little girl and I cried for my adult woman who had loved "Edward" with her whole heart. I cried, and I released. I cried and I trusted. I also received regular Reiki sessions.

Thinking back, perhaps I had to open up to Edward to begin releasing the childhood pain. Letting go of Edward also meant letting go of parts of myself that had emerged from the shadows to be healed and transformed.

This was not an easy time in my life. Edward and I saw each other a few times during this time. We were both tempted at times to reconnect sexually, but I had the clear message what would happen if we did. In those moments of weakness I reminded Edward about my dream and how if we were sexual again we would be led into initiations of fire. Neither one of us wanted this to happen. Over time we simply went our separate paths. I missed Edward deeply. I missed our spiritual connection and I missed who I was when he was in my life. I had awakened to a new awareness of who I was not only spiritually but also sexually. I'm not sure what life would have been like without the aid of Archangel Ariel. I understand how blessed I was to actually have a conscious awareness that Archangel Ariel was helping me heal my heart.

Archangel Ariel became my constant companion. Her (angels aren't male or female) energy was very soft and I experienced Archangel Ariel as pink energy rays of love. These rays of energy began the task of helping me to release emotional and physical blocks - especially the blocks/beliefs I had about letting someone love me completely.

As I worked with the energies of Ariel to heal my heart, I continued searching for my beloved. A few of the men I met had a spiritual gift to teach me. Randy was an amazing teacher as was "Tim." Tim was another man that was unavailable emotionally, but he led me into different dreams and this was when the angel Metatron came into my life as a teacher. GB came into to my life and taught me about passionate sex, uninhibited sex, spiritual, crazy, wild sex. I guess you get the point - GB taught me how to let go and I experienced many mystical moments while in his arms. GB was not available to love me completely so my search for my beloved continued.

I continued to introduce Archangel Ariel to my students and clients. The love of the angels is here to support us through the many initiations and critical choice points we experience in our lives. Again, we are not taught as children that we are incarnated souls, therefore, we are not taught that we all have spiritual companions in our lives. The Angelics have assisted many people into healing their hearts so they can bring forth more of their divine self into waking consciousness.

My relationship with my soul continued to grow and evolve. I began to understand that I was a traveler, which meant that I traveled at will through many planes of consciousness. I continued not to share this with anyone because I didn't think it was normal. There was still a part of me that wanted to fit in, to be normal. As I'm writing this book I now understand that my experiences would be defined as mystical; however, for me they were and are the norm.

By the time Archangel Metatron entered my consciousness I had already began to understand my path was the way of my soul. I didn't fully understand, but I knew that something greater than myself was leading the way. I simply had to trust the guidance I was receiving and bring my life into alignment with the path of my soul. What I've learned along the way is that most people do get the push from the world of spirit; they get the intuitive guidance but they haven't learned to trust the guidance.

Bringing one's life into alignment with the path of one's soul can shake every aspect of their life apart. This happens so it can be put back together in a way that is aligned with one's soul's life plan.

During this time Arch Angel Metatron took center stage as a teacher and guide. Arch Angel Metatron's energy was surreal. If you put the energy of a thousand angels together, you will begin to understand the force of Archangel Metatron.

Once again, I was downloaded with information and guidance. I received many spiritual activations during this time. I didn't have a teacher or anyone to explain what was occurring in my life via these activations. That said, I trusted the world of spirit and my soul. I define spiritual activations as energy which enters into our consciousness and opens the body and mind to new levels of awareness. Many of the activations we receive open key regions of our body and mind that have been doormat. Many of the activations occur during our sleep or while receiving an energy session or meditating. The spiritual activations come from God and the world of spirit and begin a rewiring process. I remind you that we are incarnated souls. We are spiritual beings; therefore, as we grow spiritually we receive spiritual activations that will open us up to new levels of consciousness both spiritually and physically.

Information from the world of spirit flooded my consciousness. I loved Metatron's energy. I now traveled to higher planes of consciousness during what I thought of as my waking state of consciousness. I was told by several spiritual teachers to be careful because many people had gotten "burnt out" by this energy or became ungrounded and forgot that Metatron's appearance in their life meant that they had been chosen to bring forth teachings of light that would help others evolve.

During this time I continued to "travel" during my daytime hours. This was a huge shift in consciousness because up until this time I only traveled while sleeping or receiving an energy session. Shifting my consciousness to other planes of consciousness became a new norm for me. Tim, was concerned that I was traveling too much and that if I kept it up I would be dead by fall. His concern was real because I began experiencing what I now know to be light body changes. I was told that I was being "rewired" physically so that I could ground more light into my body and bring forth more energy and teachings of higher light. I couldn't seem to stop myself because the mystical experiences were all consuming. Union with God was my focus, but I continued to know that a man was coming into my life. I knew our union would be spiritual in a natural way and we would love each other deeply.

In April of 2000 my dreams and traveling took on new meaning once again. I was told that I was going to experience a surge of new energy and my body had to be "rewired" once again. Reiki had opened my body and mind up and I had released major blocks; now I was being told that my body would have to be rewired in order to allow it to bring in my soul energy.

I will admit I questioned if my physical body could withstand all of the light body changes. Sometime in April I called my friend Randy and he explained I was going through what was known as Metatron's Fire. Okay, I asked Randy, what does this mean? He said that Metatron's Fire would burn away parts of my consciousness that were not in alignment with my soul's plan.

"Are you kidding?" I asked him. He said it sounds like you have been chosen to bring forth teachings of light. This is why Metatron has appeared to you.

He couldn't really explain more, but told me to trust that when Metatron's Fire occurred physically just to go to bed and let it happen. I will admit to feeling fear, but I trusted Randy and I trusted my dreams. Within a few hours of my call to Randy I began feeling like I had a fever. As the day moved on my body began to ache. I was supposed to watch my granddaughter who was six years old at the time. I tried to stay awake, but finally told her I had to go to bed. I asked Johnny to watch over her.

Looking back, I can see how the Divine Plan was once again in action. Kourt might have been six, but her soul age is very old. I remember her coming back to check on me. I had taken my temperature earlier and when I drank some water I took it again. It was 104. I knew a normal person would go to the hospital, but I was told to go back to sleep.

The fire in my spine made it feel like I was being ripped apart. I did go to sleep and went into a deep sleep as my body burned parts of my consciousness away. To be honest, I had no idea what this meant; I only knew the fire inside me felt like a real fire. It literally felt like I was being torn apart and put back together again. I didn't know if I would live to see daylight. My dreams were surreal. Every time I woke up the angels were around me. They kept telling me to sleep so I slept. I do not remember all of my dreams that night, but I know I was shown images of what was to come on earth and I was told that I would be a teacher to guide others through what my spirit teachers called the "awakening."

Once again, I trusted.

My daughter later told me that when she came to get Kourt, she was sleeping on the living room floor bundled up in a blanket and Johnny was sitting in his wheelchair watching over her. (It would be 11 years later, but Kourt was the one who helped me watch over Johnny as he birthed into spirit. They had a beautiful soul connection and Kourt now has a huge tattoo on her back which says "Johnny Angel" inside a pair of angel wings.)

When I woke up I knew I was different. This time the spiritual activations began to infuse my life with being a spiritual being. I didn't know it at the time, but I was being "reborn" as a Homospiritus. A Homospiritus physical body is capable of bringing in my light. This allows one to shine more light into the world.

I knew I wasn't the same person. I now understand that Metatron's Fire opened my consciousness, my life, to even higher levels of *walking as one with God.*

I knew that I had been changed from the inside out and that my life would never be the same. I didn't share this experience with anyone but Randy. In 1999 most people, even my students, had no conscious understanding of anything like I had just experienced. I now understand many people go through activations and soul realignments, but do so thinking they have the flu, are sick or have experienced a mental breakdown. As the weeks went by, people began asking me what had happened to "Katye." My children asked me where their mom had gone.

I was different, but I was still me.

Archangel Metatron and his teachings of light plus Metatron's Fire were activations that helped shift not only my consciousness, but also changed my physical body to receive more light. My body had survived the light body changes and rewiring and I now had a more conscious understanding that my soul was in charge of my life. My personality and my soul began working together. I had been called and I had accepted the call to be a teacher to help others move through the years which would be known to many as The Shift.

I now understand that I facilitate activations in my students during meditations and private sessions. Each student receives the activation on the level they are ready to receive it. This is the path of the modern day mystic. Spiritual activations occur naturally and spontaneously as the modern day mystic grows spiritually.

Looking back, I can clearly see the path laid out by my soul. I now know that I was born to help people move through the **SHIFT**. The Shift would not take place until the year 2012. I understood by my spiritual teachers (those in non-physical form) that the years 1998 to 2012 were the convergence years. Many who were called to be a part of the shift were also going through their own shifts of consciousness. As I write these words in the year 2016 I can see many people have gone through major shifts so that they too could be a part of the awakening.

Many were called but not everyone is able or willing to move away from fear and allow the light body changes and shifts of consciousness to occur. I realize now that it was after Metatron's Fire that I made a conscious choice to learn my life lessons through joy. Most people insist on learning their lessons via shadow energy. Shadow energy simply means energy that blocks one from seeing the light of an experience.

As I moved into the fall of 1999 I continue to ground the new me. I also continued doing "research" to find my spiritual companion.

Key Points:

1. We are spiritual beings; therefore, as we grow spiritually we receive spiritual activations that will open us up to new levels of consciousness both spiritually and physically.

2. Spiritual activations are energies which enter into our consciousness and open the body and mind to new levels of awareness.

3. Many of the activations we receive open key regions of our body and mind that have been doormats.

4. Many of the activations occur during our sleep or while receiving an energy session or meditating.

5. The spiritual activations come from God and begin a rewiring process.

6. We can learn all of our life lessons through joy and love.

Questions for Reflection:

Are you aware of any spiritual/energy activations you have received?

Are you aware that you have a team of spiritual helpers?

Do you believe you can learn your lessons through love and joy?

Are there areas of your life where you are still experiencing initiations through fire? (Learning your lessons the hard way.)

Looking back can you see how a spiritual being/an angel was a guiding force in your life?

CHAPTER EIGHT

Enchanted Love

In June of 2001 I answered an ad on an online dating site for spiritual singles. I knew without any doubt that Allan John Clark was my soul mate who was my chosen spiritual companion and lover. I had read a book called *"Enchanted Love."* I knew I would not settle for a relationship that was not enchanted. This simply meant to me that my beloved had to be willing to show up ready every day to heal those parts of self that our relationship would bring up.

In enchanted partnership both partners agree to take responsibility for their shadow parts. By taking responsibility this means that each partner takes responsibility for their thoughts and emotions. Both partners commit to showing up every day ready for enchanted love to bring them into closer reunion with God. At the core enchanted partnership is two people consciously coming together to grow spiritually while embracing physical partnership and love.

I knew that I would not settle for any relationship that was not grounded in enchantment. I hadn't realized at the time, but Edward and I experienced enchanted love because at the core of our union was our individual desire to know God.

The key words that drew me to Allan were - angels, Metatron, Reiki and spiritual journey. Not your usual words to attract a mate, but there they were. In my first email to Allan my subject title was Enchanted Love. When I hit "send" I stood up and the surge of energy that went through my body told me Allan and I had finally found each other. I remember standing up and began light weaving and speaking in tongues.

To say I was excited would be an understatement.

I knew we had found each other and I knew our journey together would open new doorways for each of us to continue to grow spiritually. I now understand that our souls were rejoicing because we found each other.

Allan and I began writing letters and talking on the phone. I knew I would have to tell him at some point that I was still legally married to Johnny. Even though I had grown and evolved my commitment to Johnny was still the same. I would cover him and shield him from the world that could not see him. Usually I waited to tell men about Johnny after I met them, but with Allan my guidance was to tell him before we met. I knew in my heart that I was ready to change my life for the right man, but I also knew I was committed to covering Johnny. He was my greatest teacher about unconditional love. I loved Johnny. We were a package deal. Anyone who loved me had to love and accept Johnny.

When I told Allan about Johnny he had a few questions, but I assured him I was ready for an enchanted relationship. Little did I know at the time that Allan and Johnny shared a soul love and bond that was as deep as the one I had with each one of them.

Allan I both understood that our union was a spiritual union. We were both clear that we were brought together to teach and to help each other grow spiritually. We were blessed that we found each other after we had each released a lot of old outdated beliefs and patterns. That's not to say that we each didn't have major growth to experience; we did and we were blessed that we were each committed to our individual growth as well as growing together as a couple.

For me, I was clear, I wanted an enchanted relationship. Allan didn't really understand what I meant by this, but he was determined to be the man to whom I would one day give my heart.

Having done major "research" to find Allan I had learned a lot about myself as a woman. One of the major things I learned was that I had to take care of my heart. It was no one else's job.

For me, taking care of my heart meant that I would no longer give my heart away to someone who didn't know what a priceless gift it was that I was giving him. Months before meeting Allan I had brought a beautiful rose quartz stone in the shape of a heart. I put the stone with a picture of Angel Ariel and asked them to hold it safely until I was ready to give it to my beloved.

Allan and I quickly began teaching together. It was as if we knew each other forever. We taught our first class together six weeks after meeting each other. We quickly found our rhythm as teachers. I smile as I remember those days. We found our sacred rhythm as teachers; now we had to see if we could find enchanted love in our personal lives.

Allan and I both grew together and we became a team. We were committed to each other and we were committed to our personal growth. My worry about Allan loving Johnny was quickly laid to rest and we settled into our rhythm as a family. Giving Allan my heart was a natural part of the journey. With each passing day I knew I could trust Allan with my heart.

Allan was my ground. With him by my side I began growing in confidence as a teacher and together we taught our students. This was another time of enchantment in my personal life as well as my life as a teacher. I loved watching my students grow and embrace their gifts. To quote Allan "life was good." We experienced enchanted love in our relationship.

We were two modern day mystics driving in a red Ford convertible and doing so while experiencing an expanded state of consciousness. Allan loved singing Doo Whops and he would light up the entire universe when he turned to me and sang. We learned that the life of the modern day mystic included joy, laughter and adventure as well as dedication to one's spiritual growth. By this time we both understood that God was to be experienced in every activity and experience. God was the core of every experience.

Throughout our journey together we continued to be committed to showing up ready to heal those parts of self that emerged from the shadows ready to be healed by love. I felt safe with Allan. I felt "covered" by his love and I know I grew into a more powerful woman because of his love.

During the years from 2002 until 2014 I continued to receive spiritual activations as well as an expanded state of consciousness. I loved the work Allan and I did together and I loved who I had grown to become. In 2006 Johnny and I were legally divorced because Allan wanted to be married to me. I know this all may sound very strange but the divorce didn't change anything in my life with Johnny. I was devoted to him and so was Allan. Allan and I loved Johnny and we loved each other. We shared a deep and abiding soul love.

During this same time period I began consciously connecting with "Anna." Anna was simply known to me as a part of my higher self. By this time it was normal for me to receive information on what to teach via my dreams. I was guided to begin a school of spiritual healing. This was an amazing time, a wonderful time of spiritual growth and expansion. I began "bringing in" teachings from Anna. Many of the teachings I shared with our students during this time were from Anna. When Allan and I had our wedding rings engraved mine said "Love Anna" and Allan's said, "Love Sethius". These were our spiritual names. I continued to grow and evolve as did Allan. The woman who had been so wounded had grown into a woman of strength, wisdom and confidence.

As time went on Johnny began growing weaker physically. In November of 2011 Johnny suffered a mild heart attack. I was with him at the time and it was terrifying. We did not call the ambulance because Johnny made a decision the year before that he wanted no more hospitals. He had seen way too many hospitals during the years. In January of 2012 he entered hospice care.

During this time I continued to see clients and Allan and I continued to teach our classes. In 2009 we had moved everything home so we could be there more with Johnny. When I was with clients it was Allan who took care of Johnny. My granddaughter Kourtney also helped with his care. In April of 2012 he became too weak to get out of bed. I wrote about his story in my book *"Birthing into Spirit."* Johnny was amazing as he shifted his consciousness to birthing into spirit. He continued to teach us until his last breath.

As I write I'm crying remembering the love we shared and the many gifts received along the way during the thirty years I spent with Johnny. He was a major teacher, friend, and soul connection. He continues to teach me and watches over me. The choice I made when I brought Johnny home had been a major choice point in my life. It shaped my entire life. There is no definition of the kind of love we shared. My life was greatly influenced and blessed by John Guy Baublitz III.

After Johnny birthed into spirit it was clear that Allan missed him as much as I did. As someone said Johnny was the heart of our family. Eighteen brain operations, heart issues, and pain from all the operations did not rob him of his essence of love. Johnny was all about love. You could not be in his presence and not be affected by his essence.

A few months after Johnny birthed into spirit my sister Debbie birthed into spirit. I share her story along with a student who birthed into spirit one year later in "Birthing Into Spirit." I believe that consciousness continues after physical death, but three people whom I loved birthing into spirit within a year was a lot, even for me.

Spiritually, I continued to grow and I knew that my life was taking a new turn. Life with Allan continued to be a time of enchantment for both of us. I was very comfortable teaching my classes and seeing my clients when Christine entered my life.

I did not know it at the time of our meeting, but Christine and I shared a soul contract, one that would change both of our lives.

Key Points:

1. At the core enchanted partnership is two people consciously coming together to grow spiritually while embracing physical partnership and love.

2. Enchanted love demands that both partners show up ready to heal the shadow parts of self that will emerge because of the relationship.

3. Soul love does not conform to the conventional rules and norms about relationships.

4. Consciousness continues after physical death, thus the term birthing into spirit.

5. Soul contracts are agreed to between souls before we are born.

Questions for Reflections:

Have you met someone and you "knew" they were going to be a part of your life? If so, who was the person and what life lessons and gifts did the experience offer?

Have you experienced enchanted love in a lover relationship?

Enchanted love begins with self. Do you show up in your life ready to be transformed or do you run away from change?

Have you experienced a relationship that did not fit into a box? If so, what kind of life lesson did it offer you?

Do you believe that life continues? If so, have you ever experienced afterlife communication with someone?

Looking back over your life can you see where you shared a soul contract with someone? If so, what was the contract?

CHAPTER NINE

The Reflector

C hristine had found our flyer and knew that we were meant to teach either her or her husband David. Somehow it was decided that David would come to our school of spiritual healing. The year was 2011. David decided to gift Christine a private session with me for Christmas. During her reading it was clear that although Christine had achieved great success as a transformational coach she was not happy. In fact, she was miserable and her life was not in alignment. When I speak about alignment I mean in alignment with the dreams and visions of our soul. After her private reading I began seeing Christine and David and they began doing the inner work that would allow them to connect at a deeper level as a couple. I must admit I was a little intimidated by Christine. She was a professional speaker and had a strong presence about her.

I had grown and evolved and I loved teaching my students but was seen as a local teacher. I was happy sitting in our circles with our students. To quote Allan, "Life was good."

During this time I continued to grow and I knew by my dreams that life as I knew it was going to change. I wasn't sure how but I knew that my life was going to change and along with it my work.

I didn't know it when I met Christine, but she is a reflector. Christine was a catalyst for me wanting more. I believe we all meet a few "Christines" throughout our lives. By this I mean someone who comes into our lives and opens us up to stepping onto the next path of bringing forth our soul's visions and dreams. This is one of Christine's core gifts. By being in her presence she reflects back to you your dreams and visions of your soul.

A reflector is a mirror. This is usually an unconscious process and is simply experienced by many people as wanting more in their life.

It had been twenty-four years since my first major soul realignment. I had grown and had experienced many shifts of consciousness since that time. I now understood that I was an incarnated soul. My soul had guided me to the place in my life where I was ready to fully embody a life that was guided and directed by my soul.

By now I understood the amazing dance we do as incarnated souls. I call it the signature dance. Our souls each have a unique soul signature. Via our soul signature we find those souls with whom we share core soul contracts. I have no doubt that my soul guided me to that nursing home when I met Johnny. Our relationship was a soul connection and I believe we shared a soul contract that brought us together when the time was right.

Do I believe that Johnny's soul created the experiences that led him to having half his brain taken out? No, I don't, but I do believe that our souls contracted to find each other in this dance we call life. Looking back, I can see many different people with whom I share a soul contract. I can clearly see the doors that were opened so that I would meet someone. Stepping onto a path to meet someone is just part of the journey. Our souls and spirit helpers can guide us to the path, but we have to choose to take the action steps that open us up to the initiation that is offered by any chosen path.

As a teacher of the soul, I now understand that our souls create a life plan and depending on the choices of the personality the life plan can take many twists and turns. Bringing the personality's life back into alignment is not an easy task for the soul.

That said, if our soul wants us to meet someone it will happen one way or another. If our life has gone too far out of alignment the world of spirit will orchestrate an initiation that is meant to help us move into alignment with the plan created by our souls. At the time of meeting someone with whom you share a core soul contract one's world can get rocked. Edward was one of those people I believe my soul guided me toward meeting, as were Johnny and Allan. This was also true about meeting Christine; our souls brought us together because of a soul agreement. A core soul agreement is, "I will be that which you have asked me to be, so you can be that which you need to be. May we seek to do this on earth in love."

It was November 18th, 2013 that my life took a dramatic shift. One morning I woke up and I was very anxious. My dreams had shown me what was about to take place. Once again, I found myself at a critical choice point. I was going through another initiation, one which would change every aspect of my life. There was no question that I would do what I was guided to do, but I didn't have to like it. Stepping onto this new path was taking me 100% out of my comfort zone. That said, by now I had grown to trust soul guidance.

I had a scheduled session with Christine. I texted her and asked if we could do a phone session. She said no, she really wanted to meet in person. I texted Allan and asked him if he would sit in on my session with Christine. He said he would but questioned why I needed him to do so. I told him I didn't want to talk about it, but I needed him by my side.

I texted Christine and told her to bring her recorder with her. Allan and I were sitting in my healing room waiting for her. When Christine walked through the door she asked me what was going on. I told her to sit down and told her to turn on the recording. I don't remember the session that day because that was the very first time that "Anna" used my voice to speak through me. Truth is Christine would not have been the person I chose to be that vulnerable in front of. Of course, this was all ego.

At the moment I allowed "Anna" to speak through me EVERYTHING in my life changed. I believe in that moment I became who I was born to be. I fully stepped into and began to embody being a Homospiritus. The many initiations, spiritual activations and critical choice points had all steered me in this direction.

I believe we are all birthing into Homspiritus. This simply means we are capable of bringing more light into our physical bodies and we know our path is one of love.

I have already shared that I had thought of Anna as a part of my higher self. I did not know until Anna started speaking through me that Anna is a group of 976 souls with whom I share a steady stream of consciousness. Anna is indeed a part of my higher self; however, my higher self includes the consciousness of 976 souls. Everything in my life changed after I allowed Anna to speak through me.

EVERYTHING.

I had known, via my dreams that I would be writing books someday, many books. After Anna started "talking" through me my sleep pattern changed. I found myself waking up around 3:00 in the morning and writing. Two weeks after my meeting with Christine I was told to stop seeing private clients.

I couldn't believe this request was being made of me. I loved seeing my private clients and saw myself doing energy work for the rest of my life.

My soul, however, had other plans, bigger plans. *I have since learned that our soul always has a bigger plan for our life than we can see. We have been taught to live in the boxes created for us by others. God and our souls do not place limits on what we can create.*

It took me about two weeks, but I stopped seeing private clients. I began writing *"Conscious Construction of the Soul."* Within six months I wrote three books. *"Into the Light"* and *"Birthing into Spirit"* were written back to back.

Before I experienced Metatron's Fire I had been told that my physical body might not be able to withstand all of the energy. In other words, the energy coming into my physical body might fry the circulatory system within me. Our current physical body is not wired to withstand such high velocity of energy. Once again, I was being asked to expand not only my consciousness, but also my physical body had to be the grounding rod for all of the energy that came along with Anna.

I knew I was going to go through more spiritual activations that would once again rewire my physical body. That said, NOTHING I had experienced in my life prepared me for what I call the DIVINE FIRE.

I received the first activation about two weeks after Anna spoke through me. I had been writing when suddenly my physical body began to feel overheated. My body began to shake and I began to feel what I can only describe as electrical charges surging through my body via my spine. I started screaming these strange sounds and moving my body. Allan came into the room and with a shocked look on his face asked what he could do to help me. I remember crying and saying, "Help me, I'm on fire."

Allan reminded me to breathe, but nothing calmed the fire that was moving down through my body. I experienced the Divine Fire Activations over a period of six months. The only thing I can closely relate it to is what people say about kundalini opening. During a Divine Fire Activation electrical energy came in through my crown chakra and seemed to travel and spread out from my spine. With each activation I merged my own consciousness with Anna, meaning the consciousness of 976 souls.

During this time Allan and I conducted healing circles called Heart Mind Gatherings. We would connect everyone via the Heart Mind and then Anna would give a discourse. We always ended the Heart Mind Gatherings with a meditation which always included some kind of energy activation.

During the first six months I didn't remember much of what Anna said, but as time went on I began integrating Anna into my consciousness. In the beginning my eyes were closed and when I opened my eyes they were very sensitive to light. I still have to have fans on me when I fully join my consciousness with Anna because my body overheats.

Allan was amazing during this time. We were like little children and couldn't wait to see what I had written during the middle of the night. We talked to Christine about my books because this was her area of expertise. When we found out that going through a traditional publisher could take years I was clear we had to self-publish.

I didn't know why but I knew I needed to get my first three books published. Allan began proof reading and putting my books in the format needed. Christine stepped in and helped with the front and back covers as well as the inside formatting. She was an amazing gift and I knew our meeting was no accident. Our souls had made a core soul agreement which is, "I will be that which you have asked me to be so that you can be that which you can be." I had grown to love Christine as I do all my students. I must admit she was very frustrating to work with at times. Thinking back, I laugh. I have no doubt that it was and is our souls that keep us both committed to growing and evolving spiritually together.

By the end of September 2014 we had published my first three books. It was clear that my soul wanted me to reach a larger audience.

Allan and I both had a reluctance to do this, but it was clear that I was now being guided to reach more students and this meant traveling to new locations around the world.

During this time the spiritual teacher in me began to emerge. Up until this time I saw myself as an energy practitioner first and teacher second. Now I fully began to step into being a teacher of soul as well as an author.

During this time Allan continued to say this was not his work. He kept telling everyone he would do more work from the other side than he was doing here. Allan's path was the path of the ascended masters. Spiritually he had grown as I had grown. We understood that although our spiritual paths merged at times, everyone is on their own individual spiritual journey. We continued to experience enchanted love. He was my best friend, my lover, and my teacher.

Life was good.

Key Points:

1. A Homspiritus is capable of bringing more light into the physical body, thus shines the light of their soul to others.

2. Via our soul signature we find those souls with whom we share core soul contracts.

3. A core soul contact is "I will be that which you have asked me to be so that you can be that which you need to be."

4. The Divine Fire is a spiritual activation.

5. A reflector is someone who reflects back to you your dreams and visions of your soul. They are the mirror. They make us want "more."

Questions for Reflections:

Have you ever met a reflector? What is the "more" they helped you to see?

Look at a few of your relationships; can you see the soul contract? How did the soul contract play out in your life?

Looking back can you think of any spiritual activations you have received? We all receive "spiritual activations" during our lives, usually after we have arrived at a critical choice point. I remind you that a spiritual activation opens your body and your mind to receiving more light/soul energy.

Are you aware of your dreams guiding you?

Have you ever experienced that instant soul recognition? If so, who was the person and what did you teach each other?

CHAPTER TEN

The Words That Changed Everything

O n November 1st, 2014 Allan and I were watching television. We were holding hands and suddenly I heard, "Katye, Allan is going to die and leave you." Three more times the voice said it again, "Katye, Allan is going to die and leave you."

I remembering looking at Allan to see if he had heard the voice; he had not. I remember thinking, "Oh my God something is going to happen and Allan is going to die." I quickly pushed what I had heard to the confines of my mind.

I knew I was being told this not to frighten me, but to prepare me. I must admit had I known how quickly the words would come true, I might have talked to Allan about them. I'm sure I would have in the morning. About thirty minutes later we went to bed and he tucked me in as he always did. He kissed me good night as he did every night and then he went to the other room to meditate. At some point I felt him lay next to me and he kissed me again.

About three hours later I woke up to go to the bathroom and realized Allan wasn't in bed. I went searching for him and found him sitting in my chair. I woke him up and asked him why he wasn't in bed. He told me he had experienced an awful headache, followed by chills and came out to the TV room so he wouldn't wake me up. I said, let's get you back to bed. We quickly realized he couldn't stand. It was then that I remembered what the voice told me, that Allan was going to die. I realized he had had a stroke. I called 911.

Allan birthed into spirit on November 4th 2014. During the days between his stroke and his birth into spirit I heard the voice again. This time I kept hearing, "Katye, it has been written." I share our story in our book called "Soul Love Never Ends." It is a book co-written by Allan after his physical death.

In our book I share my journey as I found my way through the grief and separation anxiety I experienced. I also share how Allan continues to communicate with me. It's a story of love and transformation. A few days after Allan's physical death, I realized why I felt the urgency to get the books published. Allan was so proud of our accomplishment. Had we waited to publish our books, Allan would not have held my books in his hands.

Because most people have not learned the ways of soul they only see death as an ending. The mystic understands this is a time when one must walk through the valley knowing that they are covered by God. Physical death of a loved one offers a different initiation for the modern day mystic. Keeping in mind that the mystic seeks to experience God in every experience and every activity I used this time to bring forth a rebirth of spirit in my life. To experience God as one walks through the valley of death is an initiation like none other.

After Allan's birth into spirt I found myself turning to my soul and the world of spirit to guide me. Allan had birthed into spirit. I knew that his consciousness continued. All of the initiations and critical choice points had brought me to another transitional point in my life. I didn't question why, but instead asked what do I do now? I trusted that my soul had a plan. Every day I woke up making sure to ask for help from the world of spirit. My family and friends were a constant source of strength during this time. I could feel the love of the angels covering.

During times when we move into a transitional point in our live it's a time to trust the journey. The universe is bringing everything into alignment so that you can move into the next part of your journey.

It's also a time to let go. Life as you knew it has changed. When we embrace these transitional points in our lives we begin to understand that we are moving into the energy of a rebirth. We can trust and move with the energy of change or we can hold on, digging ourselves in and fight against the change. This is the path of the modern day mystic; trusting that all is in Divine Order even when one is walking through the valley of death. I believe this is one of the defining moments in the life of a mystic.

I trusted. I reached out to the world of spirit.

I listened to the guidance I received and I allowed my soul to lead the way. I reached out to my family and community for comfort and support. I cried when I needed to cry. I slept when I needed to sleep.

Now more than ever I knew I had to trust my soul to lead me. I didn't have the plan, but I knew my soul had one.

I began working again with clients, but this time my clients called me on the phone. I began doing classes, but now they began to reach a larger audience because they were tele-classes. I did all of this while processing my grief. There was not one time that I blocked my tears or emotions. I felt every raw emotion and allowed it to be brought to the surface. I knew I had to move through the emotions or I would be swallowed up by them.

The woman who once sat at the bottom of an icy hill 32 years earlier had grown and evolved into a woman who knew that although her husband had birthed into spirit there was a plan and all was in Divine Order. I knew that God, my soul and the world of spirit would lead the way if I could stay open and allow them to do so. I had learned to walk as one with God during the many years as I moved through the many initiations, activations and crossroads. Now more than ever

I reached out to God for comfort. God was my resting place and yes, sometimes my hiding place.

During this time I continued dreaming and traveling. Many times I knew I had been with Allan when I woke up. I also began writing *"Soul Love Never Ends"* with Allan. Writing our book together helped me process my emotions, but it also opened me up to a new understanding of life after physical death. Allan continued to communicate with me. I felt blessed that I could still experience his love.

A month after Allan's birth into spirit, Christine decided to get serious about her spiritual growth. I wondered at the time if Allan's physical death was the reason for this. As a teacher of the soul, it has been my experience that many people who want to live a spiritual life are just too busy to do so.

This might sound like a strange thing to say, but we are inundated every day with experiences that take us away from the path of love. Most personalities don't take responsibility for their thoughts and emotions nor do they converge in love with others.

Many students who seek me out as their spiritual teacher have no idea how off centered their life is. This was true of Christine; she was a huge success, but had not stepped into truly being the creative force in her life. My responsibility as her spiritual teacher was to guide her into bringing ALL areas of her life into alignment with the path of love. As her spiritual teacher, I could see the real authentic Christine. As her spiritual teacher, my responsibility was to help her bring forth her authentic self, her divine self.

This of course is true for all of my students.

We began meeting by phone weekly. Our relationship was a beautiful dance as we both continued to grow and evolve. I learned many personal life lessons as I worked with Christine. She was a mirror in many ways for me. Our soul contract was a core one. She was student, teacher and daughter to me. I loved her and wanted to help her step into and fully embody her soul work. I continue to be her spiritual teacher and she continues to be a guiding force in my life. Ours is a sacred dance.

I personally believe every relationship is teacher-student. Meaning we all have something to teach and to learn from one another, even our children. Relationships are a beautiful dance, a sacred dance between souls. My relationship with Christine has opened us both up to wanting more in many different areas. I feel blessed that we have found each other and that together we will reach others through our messages of love.

During this time I also continue to merge my consciousness with Anna. I was now one with this group of 976 souls. We truly shared a steady stream of consciousness. The Divine Fire Activations I experienced a year earlier only happened occasionally now. My body was adapting to Anna's energy. This was truly a blessing.

Life was good. I continued to heal my heart as I also began to focus on getting my soul teachings out to the world. The only downside was my books were not being read by the millions of people I thought they would reach. That said, I continued to receive guidance to continue writing and teaching. I woke up every day embracing that I am the creative force in my life. I consciously choose to allow joy to guide me. I also experienced Grace in my life in profound ways as I continued to grow and evolve.

The teacher of the soul was emerging in me. I now knew that I was a teacher of souls. This meant that I had to find a way to teach about soul in a way that my students would be able to understand. By the summer of 2015 my work continued to expand and I found myself teaching Mind Mastery and Life Mastery. I knew that many teachers of soul shy away from teaching about the afterlife and pre-life of the soul, but I knew as a teacher of soul I had to help my students understand the vastness of what they truly are as incarnated souls.

I began to learn how to engage social media and because three of my books were about birthing into spirit people began identifying me with grief. I knew I was reaching people with my birthing into spirit writings, but I wanted to help people embrace that they are incarnated souls. I wanted to teach people tools that would help them empower their lives. When the anniversary of Allan's birth into spirit came I knew that my life was in alignment with my soul and that I was on the pathway I needed to be on to continue bringing forth the teachings of my soul.

I also knew as time went on I would feel the pull to experience enchanted love once again. I do not believe that there is only one great love in our lives. I had already experienced enchanted love with three beautiful men. I remain certain that when the time is right, I will be led into the path where I will meet my beloved. Who knows, perhaps I'm already on that path even now as I write this book.

Key Points:

1. The world of spirit prepares us for life changing events. For me it was hearing a voice preparing me that Allan was going to die.

2. When we embrace these transitional points in our lives, we begin to understand that we are moving into energy of a rebirth.

3. We can trust and move with the energy of change or we can hold on, digging ourselves in and fight against the change.

4. During times when we move into a transitional point in our life, it's a time to trust the journey.

5. During transitional points in your lives the universe is bringing everything into alignment so that you can move into the next part of your journey.

6. Every relationship is teacher-student. Meaning we all have something to teach and to learn from one another, even our children.

7. Relationships are a beautiful dance, a sacred dance between souls.

Questions for Reflections:

Have you ever received a message about something that was going to happen? If so at the time of receiving the message did you believe it?

During times of great change do you trust the journey of change and endings or do you try to hold onto life as it is?

Looking back can you pick out a few key relationships that taught you a core life lesson? If so, what were the lessons. Did you learn the lesson through ire or Grace? Do you now understand the soul lessons?

Can you identify major teachers in your life?

Part Two

The Teachings
of Katye Anna

CHAPTER ELEVEN

I AM Who
I Was Born To Be

E very life lesson, initiation, activation and critical choice point I experienced during my life opened/awakened me up to embracing the divine in every experience. My entire life has prepared me to step into and fully embody being a teacher of soul. As a teacher of soul, I seek to teach my students what their tribe and elders did not teach them. The first thing I teach my students is that they are an incarnated soul. As an incarnated soul, we have the very spark of God within us. I teach my students the language of the soul and how to embrace being a modern day mystic. As a teacher of soul it is my responsibility to awaken the mystic within my students and to help them see their life through the lens of spiritual consciousness.

I also teach my students the power of choice. The truth is we make many choices every day and most of them are made unconsciously. When we understand the power of choice we begin to see that every choice we make, consciously or unconsciously has the possibility of affecting our lives for years and even a lifetime.

Each choice is a stepping stone to the next choice.

As a teacher of soul I teach my students "The Three Spiritual Keys for Empowered Soulful Living." I offer several pathways that teach my students how to fully embrace the magnificence of their souls. Everything I teach has been created from the pathway I followed during my life. Of course thirty-four years ago I had no conscious understanding that my soul was leading me, nor did I know that I was an incarnated soul.

In sharing my journey I could clearly see how I had lived an unconscious life until I had that first soul realignment in 1987. The truth is most people live their life unconsciously. We do this because our tribe did not teach us that we are the creative force in our lives. As a teacher of soul it is my responsibility to wake you up and help you begin creating your life from a place of empowerment. I was forty years old before I really began to understand that through the power of choice I created my life. As a teacher of soul, I teach conscious living, conscious loving and conscious dying.

My *Life Mastery Program* is my signature year-long tele-program which gives my students the tools and resources they need to shift from creating their lives unconsciously to creating their lives and their experiences consciously fueled by the wisdom and guidance of their soul. During *Life Mastery* I help each student embrace that nothing happens in their life that they haven't agreed to. This isn't as easy as it might sound. Because many people are invested in staying in their wounds. My responsibility is understanding what my student's process is and what old outdated beliefs and patterns are fueling their life. Taking responsibility for that which we have created opens the student onto the path of the mystic for the mystic understands that God is in every experience and every activity. Embracing this core belief that we are each responsible for everything we are creating takes many on an initiation of transformation that will empower the mystic's life should they choose to allow it to do. Releasing old outdated beliefs and patterns becomes a way of life for the modern day mystic. I teach my students how to move from learning life lessons through the initiations of fire into learning life lessons through the initiations of grace and of love. The modern day mystic begins to understand that living a spiritual life isn't something we do, but is a way of "being" in the world.

As one embraces that they are a spiritual being, all of the senses are heightened and intuition begins to be a guiding force in one's life. The power of choice and knowing that we are each responsible for that which we are creating takes the modern day mystic onto a path of self-discovery and awareness. Taking responsibility for that which we are creating takes the modern day mystic into a new awareness of what it means to be the creative force in one's life.

I love watching my students embrace who they were born to be. My job is not to tell my students who I know they already are but to lead them into embracing who they are. They do this by living what I teach them via discourses and meditations. The homework is implementing a few key spiritual practices and teachings into their lives.

As a teacher of soul I teach my students how to empower their lives by letting go of old outdated beliefs and patterns. I woke up one day with the words "catch and release" and my Mind Mastery program was born. Once again, I was guided by my dreams to teach what is now known as "catch and release."

My *Mind Mastery* is my foundation program. Mind Mastery's focus is teaching students how to "catch and release" old outdated beliefs and patterns that block you from fully stepping into and creating your life empowered by your soul. The ***Three Keys for Empowered Soulful Living*** were also given to me during my dreams. They are simple, but not always easy to follow. When using the Three Keys you will begin moving through your initiations in love. You take responsibility for the energy you bring into every experience. You embrace the connectedness of all life, meaning you will begin to understand that we all connected and can only succeed together.

The Three Keys for Empowered Soulful Living

Key One: Converge with others in love.

Key Two: Take responsibility for your thoughts and your emotions.

Key Three: We can only succeed together.

I believe by incorporating these three spiritual keys into your life you will begin to create experiences of love and experiences that empower your life. You will still go through initiations, but by changing your thoughts about any experience you will change the experience itself, thus the initiation.

Your life has been shaped by many initiations. Like me, you might have experienced many of your initiations through fire, meaning the hard way. Most likely you were not aware of the critical choice points and transitional points you experienced in your life. During your life you have received many spiritual activations that have helped you during your journey on earth. Most of these spiritual activations and initiations went unnoticed by you. You simply thought you had the flu or a cold. You rested a few days and then went on with life.

Embracing that you are a modern day mystic opens you and your life up to new awareness and new possibilities as you embrace that you have the power of choice and that you are the creative force behind your life. You will begin to see your life in a new way. Life experiences will be seen as initiations. Spiritual activations will be recognized, as will the critical choice points in your life.

I believe by reading my book you have arrived at a transitional point in your life. Truth is you wouldn't be reading this book if you were not ready to step onto a new path.

There are many pathways you have taken on your journey. If you have answered the questions for reflection at the end of each chapter, hopefully you are beginning to understand that the power of God is within you and that you can change the circumstances of your life. Remember, your soul will use every initiation as a way of helping you move into embracing that you are the creative force in your life. Your life experiences have not randomly happened to you. Everything in your world has been agreed to by you, be it at a soul level or a personality level. Until you embrace this core spiritual truth you will continue to believe that life happens TO you.

Nothing happens TO you. You have made an agreement to allow the experience into your life. There are several core initiations that every personality experiences. One is childhood; during childhood your soul entrusted you to the care your tribe. Every personality has several opportunities to heal the wounds of childhood. This initiation will present itself over and over again and will touch every relationship you have until you have courage to move beyond the wounds and old outdated beliefs and patterns of childhood.

The choice is yours.

It always has been.

When you make the choice to move away from the circumstances and initiations of childhood your life will take on new meaning. You will begin to see through the eyes of the mystic; in doing so you will be able to see God even in your childhood initiations and experiences. When this happens, you have stepped onto the path that will lead you into new initiations that will empower your life and the lives of everyone you touch.

Key Points:

1. When we understand the power of choice we begin to see that every choice we make has the possibility of affecting our lives for years and even a lifetime. Each choice is a stepping stone to the next choice.

2. Nothing happens TO you because you have made an agreement to allow the experience into your life.

3. Living a spiritual life isn't something we do, but is a way of "being" in the world.

4. There are several core initiations that every personality experiences. One is childhood

5. The power of choice and knowing that we are each responsible for that which we are creating takes the modern day mystic onto a path of self-discovery and awareness.

Questions for Reflections:

Looking back in your life can you see how the power of choice has affected your life?

Can you see times when your guidance tried to guide you one way but you chose to stay the course? Looking back can you see how staying on the same path brought more life experiences through the initiations of fire?

As you reflect upon your life can you see how you continued learning the same life lesson over and over again until you chose to do something different?

Do you agree with the statement that we are each responsible for the life we have created?

CHAPTER TWELVE

Angels Guiding The Way

In sharing my journey I think it's apparent that I believe in angels. I believe we all share a connection to the world of spirit and spirit beings. These spirit beings make themselves known to us in ways that work within our tribal experiences. Looking back over my life I can clearly see how my angelic companions helped me move through the many initiations and activations I experienced. Ariel, Michael, Metatron, Sarah, Daniel, Raphael, and Gabriele are a few angels who have guided me and helped me during my life. Of course they did not give themselves these names. That said, each angel has their own unique energy that they shine upon our lives. Even when I had no conscious awareness that my spirit helpers were guiding my life they were doing so; this is true for you also. Your spirit team of helpers may be very different than mine. I believe by teaching you about a few of my angelic companions you will begin to invite yours to be made known to you.

We are NEVER alone. During every initiation and crossroads of our lives we are surrounded by our very own team of spirit helpers and our soul. At every crossroads there was an angel guiding me, encouraging me. I didn't know thirty-four years ago, but the *"energy"* I felt pushing me to end my marriage and to drive up that icy hill was my soul and my team of spirit helpers. Even though I had no conscious awareness of being guided by my soul, it guided me none the less. Through our dreams, thought transmissions and signs the world of spirit is constantly communicating with us. It never stops; even when the personality has no awareness of being guided the world of spirit will continue to do so.

Having free will we have to make a choice to follow the dreams and subtle messages or to keep pushing them to the side. The choice is ours.

Throughout our lives, we receive guidance and soul direction. As a teacher of soul, I believe by teaching you how to tune in and pay attention to the world of spirit you will begin to see the initiations, paths, and activations in your own life.

Messages from spirit are often very subtle because we have not developed this connection. When you begin to understand the language of the soul and the world of spirit you will begin to see, feel, and hear what has always been happening around you.

Everyone is born connected to the world of spirit via their spiritual guidance system; however, the chatter from the outer world and the tribe begins to overwhelm the child and the focus is quickly placed on the outer world. The good news is it is never too late to open up to your spiritual guidance system, thus beginning to hear the world of spirit.

Beings of light are experienced by every culture. They are called by many different names, but spiritual beings have traveled with us on earth from the dawn of our creation. I call them angels.

The world of spirit guides you in many different ways. Some of you "sense" the world of spirit. Some of you "hear" the world of spirit and some of you "see" the world of spirit. This is a good base to begin building your spiritual guidance system.

Here are a few ways you have all experienced the world of spirit. You "see" a light flicker out of the corner of your eye. You "sense" that you are not alone in the room. You have "felt" an energy of warmth across your face, shoulders, hands, or arms. You "felt" as if you've just been hugged. The air pressure often changes when a spiritual being enters the room. The room temperature may seem to shift, or you might catch a whiff of a beautiful fragrance that you can't quite identify. When the angels hug you, you feel a warmth flow through your entire body and your heart expands with a feeling of unconditional love. You "hear" a message to call a friend or not to go down a certain road. You "think" about someone and they call you. You have a dream about someone who has birthed into spirit (died a physical death) and you wake up with a sense of peace. You wake up with the answer about an experience you had been struggling with before going to sleep. You wake up with a longing to change your life. You "hear" a thought repeated over and over again in your mind. These "thoughts" encourage you to change your life in a major way.

As you reconnect with the world of spirit you begin to pay attention to these thoughts, feelings, dreams, and guidance in ways that begin to empower your life.

Because we are incarnated souls, we were born connected to the world of spirit. As children, we had some kind of awareness that we have spirit companions. Every child has a few "imagery" friends. Many people ask why children don't talk about seeing angels. They don't talk about the pictures on the wall, because they are simply a part of the landscape; this is true with spiritual beings - they are just a part of the child's world. Fortunately, our spirit companions do not go away simply because we do not acknowledge their presence in our lives.

I believe we each have six to eight major choice points during our adult years. When you understand these major choice points occur after a series of initiations you will begin to see a rhythm to your life. As a modern day mystic you will begin to understand that every initiation, every experience has brought you to a crossroad where you, the mystic, the incarnated soul, has a choice to make. You will be supported by the world of spirit in whatever choice you make.

Hopefully as you read this book and answered the questions for reflection you have begun to see the many initiations, crossroads and activations you have received along the way. Perhaps looking back you can see the many signs you received to change a relationship, job, move, etc.

One of the ways to strengthen your spiritual guidance system is to begin to pay attention and follow the "guidance" you receive. Trusting and acting on your spiritual guidance system begins to connect you with your intuitive mind.

Spiritual consciousness shifts the focus from experiencing your life via physical consciousness. Physical consciousness is what your tribe taught via your five senses of smell, taste, touch, sight, and hearing. Your sixth sense which is intuition was never developed and in many cases your sixth sense of intuition was humanized out of you by the time you could formulate your tribe's language.

I hope that you are beginning to understand that your spiritual guidance system has always been communicating with you via your senses, through transmissions and your dreams. I suggest you keep a journal over the next month as you begin to expand your connection with your spiritual guidance system.

You begin to expand your spiritual guidance system by taking the focus off of the physical world and experiences. You do this by creating space in your life for the world of spirit.

You must create an environment where you are free to explore the ways of the soul. This includes releasing the old outdated beliefs that you are not intuitive. Everyone has an intuitive mind; you simply were not taught how to develop it. The great news is you can begin today to create an environment that will help you to connect with and listen to the guidance of your intuitive mind.

Begin by honoring that you are a multidimensional being and that you are expanding the consciousness of God. As a modern day mystic begin to see your life through the lens of energy. Everything you experience has an energy signature.

You must allow time EVERYDAY in your busy schedule to communicate with the world of spirit. You were taught by your tribe to see everything via the lens of physical consciousness. This will require dedication as you move your focus into see EVERY experience via spiritual consciousness.

Stop asking WHY and start asking what am I to learn from this experience?

Ask yourself what do I have to teach others about love via this experience?

You must allow space and time to understand the language of spirit. This means learning the ways you have already developed how you "see" "hear" and "sense" the world of spirit.

Everyone has spirit guides and teachers. Begin to know your team by making time to get to know them.

Here is an angel Chart to help you get started. These are a few of the angels I have called on to assist me.

Angel	Color/Energy Ray	
Archangel Ariel	Pink energy ray	Call on Ariel in times of heartache. Ask Ariel to help you release the heartache.
Archangel Raphael	Emerald Green	Call on Raphael for healing of the physical body.
Archangel Gabriel	Turquoise	Call on Gabriel to help you speak your truth in love.
Archangel Daniel	Yellow	Call on Daniel when you need help forgiving yourself or someone else.
Archangel Michael	Indigo	Call on Michael when you are experiencing fear of any kind. Ask him to illuminate your eyes so you can see clearly

Key Points:

1. We are NEVER alone.

2. During every initiation and crossroads of our lives we are surrounded by our very own team of spirit helpers and our soul.

3. Everyone is born connected to the world of spirit via their spiritual guidance system, however the chatter from the outer world and the tribe begins to overwhelm the child and the focus is quickly placed on the outer world.

4. Through our dreams, thought transmissions and signs the world of spirit is constantly communicating with us.

5. You begin to expand your spiritual guidance system by taking the focus off of the physical world and experiences.

6. As you reconnect with the world of spirit you begin to pay attention to these thoughts, feelings, dreams, and guidance in ways that begin to empower your life.

7. The world of spirit guides you in many different ways. Some of you "sense" the world of spirit. Some of you "hear" the world of spirit and some of you "see" the world of spirit.

Questions for Reflection:

Are you ready to embrace that you have a team of spirit helpers?

Have you experienced the presence of an angel or spirit guide in your life?

In what ways do you experience the world of spirit? Do you "hear" messages? Do you "feel" the presence of the world of spirit? Do you see the world of spirit? (Many you can catch the world of spirit out of the corner of your eye as a bright white spot of light.)

When you receive information in the form of intuition do you follow it or push it aside?

Do you create room in your busy life for the world of spirit?

CHAPTER THIRTEEN

The Signature Dance

*The Law of Vibration states that everything in the universe is
in a constant state of vibration. We are vibrational beings and
we are constantly communicating with the universe and other
personalities via vibrational signatures. The dance of signatures
begins from the moment we are born. This dance of signatures
is a sacred dance, a beautiful dance. We will teach you now
about your personality's vibrational signature and your soul
vibrational signature.*

F inding one another in the physical world takes great
planning on a soul level. This is why we have two key
signatures that will greatly influence our lives. We have
a soul signature and a vibrational signature.

When we meet someone, even as an infant, there is
instant soul recognition because every soul has a unique soul

signature. This is often an intuitive knowing. Looking back, I can clearly see how I "knew" Johnny by our soul signatures. Despite the fact that I had just ended my marriage and I was unsure of the path I was on, when I met Johnny I knew him. I now understand that the "knowing" was because I knew his soul and he knew mine.

As I think back on my life I can clearly see the personalities with whom I experienced an instant soul recognition. I smile thinking about the students that I have met. Many of them how found me during times of great change and stress in their lives. In this great big world we found each other. This is the signature dance. Our souls will find each other when the timing is right. This may not be apparent at the time, especially if our life is rocked by the meeting of another soul as it was in my life when I met Edward. When I met Edward those many years ago I wasn't looking to change my life, at least on a conscious level, but my soul knew it was time to take me onto another path for soul growth and soul expansion.

We meet someone and the signature dance begins because our souls share a soul contract and a soul signature. When we meet someone as an adult soul recognition of another, often changes our lives in powerful ways. Of course, soul recognition is often only a temporary knowing that can be quickly pushed aside because we have not been taught that we are incarnated souls. We would be wise to pay attention when we meet someone and experience a direct knowing of them, for this person has something major to teach us about love.

Your personality also has a core vibrational signature. Your personality's vibrational signature affects every choice we make, every initiation we experience and critical choice point we experience during our lives.

During the age from birth until six years old your personality's core vibrational signature was formed. Your personality's core vibrational signature contains the beliefs and agreements that becomes the driving force in which you create your experiences, thus your life.

When you were born one of the reasons you slept a lot was so that your body and the spark of your soul could have time to merge. As an infant you had on-going soul communication. You were also assessing the physical world around you via your energy field.

Take a moment and think about this.

Before you were even two years old you had determined what the energy of your tribe was. During this time of development you had an ongoing connection with the world of spirit. Your tribe had forgotten the soul contracts and did not create a world where you could explore through all of your senses. They taught you how to speak the language of the tribe and the skills you would need in the physical world. Your family did not open space within the tribe for you to move into and expand the consciousness of the tribe. They forgot that you were here to teach them as well as learn from them. You were expected to fit into the tribe as it was before you were born.

Before you were two years old you had determined what was going on in your tribe and what role your tribe needed you to play. Many people continue to play these roles, even as adults because they have no knowledge of the role their vibrational single plays in their lives.

Everyone's vibrational signature contains core beliefs and thoughts. These core beliefs and thoughts are projected out into the world and attracts other personalities into your experiences. These core beliefs and thoughts are also sent out to the universe which is your partner in co-creating on earth.

This is the way you invite experiences and people into your life, via your vibrational signature.

Via your vibrational signature you "send out" messages to others.

Unknowingly, you began a "signature dance" via your vibrational signature and you attracted, thus invited, other people and experiences into your life. As I shared my journey you can clearly see how the signature danced played out with several key people.

We are doing this signature dance consciously or unconsciously. Because you are a vibrational being your signature dance began even before you could speak the language of the tribe. Many of your childhood experiences occurred because of your tribe's core vibrational signature. It was the responsibility of your tribe to keep you safe. Because patterns of behaviors fuel the lives of all members of the tribe your experiences as a child were largely influenced by the ongoing life lessons those in your tribe were experiencing before you were born.

If you want to understand the vibrational signature of your tribe during your childhood years just look at your childhood experiences.

The good news is that was then and this is now. Old outdated beliefs and patterns can be changed.

Change your vibrational signature and you will change your life.

To begin understanding your core vibrational signature, the messages you are sending out to others and the universe, begin to look at your life as it is today. We remind you that the experiences and people in your life have been invited in by your vibrational signature.

The life of the awakened modern day mystic understands the power behind living a life of daily reflection. Begin today by reflecting on your life. Can you see the messages your vibrational signature is sending out? Remember, people are always showing up in your life to give you the experiences you are asking for based on your vibrational signature.

What initiations and experiences are you asking for currently?

Remember, you have been transmitting your vibrational signature since birth. Although your vibrational signature is in constant motion, thus changing, the universe will pick up the strongest messages sent forth from your signature. Many times these messages are stored in the subconscious programing therefore you can be transmitting messages unconsciously.

This is why many people are confused by current day experiences of their life. Their everyday experiences are not in alignment with their current beliefs. The universe sends you the experience you have asked for consciously or unconsciously. Remember, you are on auto pilot 90% of your waking day. This means that outdated beliefs and patterns will have major influence over your life until you release them from the subconscious mind and your vibrational signature.

As personalities we will live the majority of our lives on autopilot. You may know consciously that you are a powerful man/woman, but if you are holding onto old outdated beliefs from childhood you must reprogram the subconscious mind to transmit programs that are in alignment with love.

You tribe did not encourage you to bring forth the creative expression of your soul because they were never taught to bring forth their own creative expression of their own souls. For the most part you were expected to fit into the box which contained the core beliefs of the tribe at the time of your birth.

You have spent most of your life trying to adapt to the ways of the world around you. *You were born to change the world, not fit into a world which had forgotten the way of love.*

If you want to change your life, you have to change your vibrational signature. You are the creative force in your life.

The choice is yours.

You can continue creating your life the way you have been or you can step onto a new path that will lead you into a life of self-discovery and transformation.

If you're ready to change your vibrational signature begin today by living a conscious life and embracing that you are an incarnated soul.

You must also take command over your life and "Catch and Release" old outdated beliefs and patterns that are bringing you experiences that are not in alignment with love.

Key points from this chapter:

1. Everything in your world has its own vibration.

2. We have two key signatures that will greatly influence our lives. We have a soul signature and a vibrational signature.

3. Soul recognition is that instant "knowing" of someone when we meet them. This is often an intuitive knowing.

4. We would be wise to pay attention when we meet someone and experience a direct knowing of them, for this person has something major to teach us about love.

5. You have a vibrational signature, which holds beliefs and patterns you agree to from birth to age six.

6. Your vibrational signature transmits the energy of you.

7. You attract, thus invite, other people and experiences into your life via the dominating beliefs and patterns contained within your vibrational signature.

8. You were born to change the world, not fit into a world which has forgotten the way of love.

9. Moving away from one's wounds is a deliberate act of self-love.

Questions for Reflection:

Have you ever met someone and felt like you knew them? If yes, looking back, what experience entered into your life when you met this person?

Looking back can you identify the many different people with whom you share a major soul contract?

Have you ever made a decision to change your life and in doing so rocked the world of someone else?

Looking back can you see how the soul agreement "I will be that which you have asked me to be so that you can be that which you need to be" has been the guiding force of the experience?

In what ways have you been trying to fit into the world? I also call this playing small. In what ways have you been playing small in your life?

CHAPTER FOURTEEN

The Three Spiritual Keys

I didn't know it at the time, but many years earlier after I had my soul realignment I began to catch and release old outdated beliefs and patterns. Releasing old outdated beliefs and patterns changes one's vibrational signature, which changes one's life. During the years of therapy and receiving Reiki sessions I began to release and let go of childhood wounds. I began to learn about the power of affirmations. Looking in the mirror and telling myself that I loved myself became a way of life.

During my years as an energy healer, I helped my students catch and release old outdated beliefs and patterns.

In 2015 when I launched my Mind Mastery Program, "Catch and Release" was officially born. **Catch and release is a very effective way of taking command over old outdated beliefs and patterns which are stored in the subconscious mind.**

The subconscious mind is the hard drive and stores and backs up each old outdated belief. Your physical body also stores memory. Releasing old outdated beliefs and patterns demands your full attention.

For the most part we live unconscious, robotic lives. We are on autopilot about 90% of our day. Take a moment and think about this statement.

90% of your waking experiences you go on to auto pilot and move through your life doing much of what you did the day before. Everyone who has ever driven a car can recall driving from point A to point Z and not remembering every detail. This may be great while driving, but living your life on autopilot fueled by old outdated beliefs and patterns will keep you living your life on the bridge to nowhere.

You know you're on the bridge to nowhere when you find yourself creating the same experiences over and over again. All of the resolve, determination and will power will not move you from the bridge to nowhere if you have not cleared out the subconscious programing from childhood.

Using the simple but specific p rocess o f M ind Mastery will put you in the driver's seat of your life.

Mind Mastery teaches you what your tribe didn't teach you. You are the creative force in your life. Mind Mastery requires your FULL participation in your life. This might sound like a strange thing to say, but because we live 90% of our lives on autopilot the "you" that is showing up in your life could be a wounded six year old. This is why your full, conscious participation in your life is required.

Mind Mastery requires that you take responsibility for the energy you bring into EVERY situation. YOU are responsible for every choice that you make, be it consciously or unconsciously.

Mind Mastery is built upon The Three Spiritual Keys for Empowered Soulful Living.

Key One: "Converge with others in love." If the situation, relationship, or experience is not one of love move your energy away from it. It is this simple and yet even to see that an experience is in alignment with love or not requires you to be consciously aware. A key question one must make when determining if the experience is in alignment with love is to ask oneself if anyone is being harmed, be it emotionally, physically and or spiritually by the experience. This includes yourself. Of course, this isn't always clear.

When I ended my marriage thirty-four years ago I set myself free. In doing so, I also set my ex-husband free to find happiness with someone who could love him the way he needed to be loved. Today we are friends and I can say I love him and his beautiful wife. By moving away from an experience that is not in alignment with love, we set foot on a new path, one that has the opportunity to transform everyone involved in the experience. Of course, everyone has to choose which path they will step onto when they come to a crossroad in their life. Sometimes we arrive at a critical choice point because someone has chosen for us. This was the case with my first husband and yet he stepped onto a new path and transformed his life with the power of choice. He chose to learn and grow from our time together.

Every day personalities are creating experiences thinking they are acting in love. An example of this is taking a stand for a cause that is not in alignment with love. Peace will never be experienced for long if it was achieved by war against another. I know that this statement will cause confusion because for eons personalities have harmed others in the pursuit of shifting consciousness or creating change. Key one requires us to converge with others in love. This requires a consciousness shift because love is not demanding, love is not impatient, love is not selfish, and yet we live in a world that is all of these things and more.

How does one change one's life by converging in love? Those many years ago when I ended my marriage, it was the loving thing to do. When I ended my relationship with my partner it was the loving thing to do because I could no longer show up in integrity. Harm is often inflicted in another not by the action one takes when ending a relationship but by the reaction of the other person in the experience. Harm is often created when we stay in a relationship because we are afraid to hurt them or of the change that will occur when ending a connection with someone.

Our lives are constantly changing. When confronted with the initiation of change we often feel as if it's being forced on us by another. Perhaps this is sometimes true.

I believe the core soul contract, "I will be that which you have asked me to be, so you can be that which you need to be. May we seek to do this on earth in love" is the guiding force in our lives during times of great change. The energy of soul moves us into action and our lives are forever changed as are the lives of those involved in the initiation of change.

The modern day mystic learns how to enter into the initiation of change understanding it as an opportunity for transformation.

Love is at the core of every experience, even when it is not apparent to us. Remember, the journey of the modern day mystic is to experience God in every experience and activity.

There will be many experiences where fear will try and be your guide for an experience. Fear and love cannot abide in the same time space continuum. It is simply impossible.

Your job is to move your consciousness to a place of love. Many of you are saying this is impossible. No, it isn't, but it takes your full participation in being responsible for your thoughts and your emotions. Many of us have old outdated beliefs that have triggers attached to them. These triggers when pushed, will set off a rush of emotions. Your responsibility is to be conscious and when you have been triggered YOU must take command of your thoughts and your emotions.

When triggered it is your responsibility to return to a place of love.

Key Two: "Take responsibility for your thoughts and your emotions." **This simply means that when an** experience has pushed a trigger or is not in alignment with love you must "Catch and Release." To catch and release you follow a few simple but very specific steps.

Step One: As soon as you know that you have been triggered or have been pulled into an experience that is not in alignment with love, you must move out of the energy, thus the experience.

Begin taking a few deep breaths. The breaths will begin to help your body/mind relax. Remember, when you have been triggered or are in an experience that is not in alignment with love 99.9% of the time fear has kicked in. This means that your body/mind moves into survival mode. Fight or flight kicks in and your body is put on hyper alert. Your HPA axis kicks in and your body is flooded with hormones meant to help you survive the "attack." **By catching your breath and connecting with your breath you will begin to alert your body/mind that you are safe.**

If you are with someone when an old outdated belief comes up and you have been triggered the next step you must take is moving out of the energy, thus the experience. This simply means you excuse yourself and go to the bathroom, go for a walk, or do whatever you can, in the moment, so you can begin the process of catching and releasing.

If you cannot excuse yourself, you can say to yourself that you know that you have been triggered by an experience or/an old outdated belief and that you are taking command over emotions that are flooding through your mind and body. Use your breath to move you away from the rush of emotions that are producing a chemical reaction in your body.

Once you have moved out of the energy you can "catch" whatever has been triggered by the old outdated belief or experience. This will usually take a few moments. Ask for help from your guides. It can be as simple as saying, "I've been triggered and I need help to understand what the old outdated belief is."

Remember, we have thousands of old outdated beliefs stored so it may take you a few moments to CATCH which ones are coming out of the shadows to be transformed.

When you do not take command over your **thoughts and emotions you will be pulled into the experience, down the rabbit hole, and into the fire.** Initiations of fire will continue to be the way you learn your life lessons until you take command over your thoughts, emotions and your life.

Remember, nothing gets transformed by being pulled into an experience that is not in alignment with love. Initiations of fire always pull you into the rabbit hole. Nothing gets transformed by the light when you get pulled into the shadow land of an experience. NOTHING!

When you have a clear understanding of what you need to release you simply affirm that this old outdated belief, person, experience, has no power over you. You say, "I release it here and now." (You can name whatever it is that you are releasing,) I personally like to give it to Archangel Michael. Whatever works for you, is the right way to release. As you can see by my journey, angels have been a part of my life. Asking them for help is like asking my best friend to help me.

When you begin to take command over your thoughts and your emotions you will begin to understand the power behind the words, "you are the creative force in your life."

NOTHING happens in your life that you have not made some kind of agreement with it being true.

Remember the majority of your beliefs were imprinted before you were six years old. These beliefs are what you have created ALL of your experiences.

Over time you will begin to catch and release automatically.

Key Three: "We can only succeed together." Most likely the core people in your life today, unless they are a part of your tribe, were not responsible for the old outdated beliefs and patterns. That said they love you enough to be that which you need them to be so that you can be that which your soul has created you to be. In other words, they will be the mirror you need to be the incarnated soul of love that you came here to be.

You are an incarnated soul, thus you are a multidimensional being. This means that you have the entire resources of the universe to heal you. This also means that what you create here on earth will touch the lives of everyone on earth.

We cannot succeed without each other.

We are in a critical choice point time here on earth. We have been here many times before.

The choice is simple: you either stand in love or fear.

Many of you have lived your lives going back and forth between experiences of love and fear. The times we are living in demands that you create your experiences in love. Many experiences will try to push you into initiations of fear. It is your responsibility to catch and release the fear.

As seen from the higher planes of consciousness we can see pockets on earth where love is permeating the world. Do not be discouraged by current experiences on earth. Your responsibility is to continue creating experiences of love.

Call forth the power of your soul to guide you. Call forth the legions of light beings who are ready to help.

Create all of your experiences using the Three Spiritual Keys for Empowered Living and you will begin to see your world and the world transformed to a place of love.

To merge your soul's visions and dreams into your current vibrational signature will take *deliberate action* on your part. As the creative force in your life, you must become aware of old outdated beliefs and patterns and begin to catch and release them.

Awareness of your major old outdated beliefs and patterns is a first step. *Awareness* alone will not change your vibrational signature. *Deliberate action is the catch and release part of the process along with creating a new empowering belief.* In the beginning of the "catch and release" process your vibration signature is not strong enough to hold the new vibrational signal and this is why affirmations help once you catch and release the old outdated believe the patterns. An affirmation is a power statement -one which reinforces the new belief. Every time you do catch and release with an old outdated belief and pattern it begins to tear away at the energetic fabric of that which created the vibrational signature. The gift of catch and release is one day you realize that you no longer get your button pushed or get pulled into the drama. This is how you know that the old outdated belief has been released. This is how you change your vibrational signature.

Remember, every day is a brand new day. Every day you have the opportunity to show up in your life knowing that you have the spark of God within. You are expanding the very consciousness of God.

Key Points:

1. Catch and release is a very effective way of taking command over old outdated beliefs and patterns which are stored in the subconscious mind.

2. Your vibrational signature is the way you communicate with the world around you.

3. The subconscious mind is the hard drive and stores and backs up each old outdated belief. Your physical body also stores memory. Releasing old outdated beliefs and patterns demands your full attention.

4. To change your vibrational signature you must catch and release old outdated beliefs and patterns. Mind Mastery requires that you take responsibility for the energy you bring into EVERY situation. YOU are responsible for every choice that you make, be it consciously or unconsciously.

5. The modern day mystic learns how to enter into the initiation of change understanding it as an opportunity for transformation.

6. The Three Spiritual Keys for Empowered Soulful Living.

Key One: Converge with others in love.

Key Two: Take responsibility for your thoughts and your emotions.

Key Three: We can only succeed together.

Questions for Reflection:

Are you aware of how old outdated beliefs and patterns have fueled your life?

What current old outdated belief are you ready to catch and release?

Do you take responsibility for your triggers, your wounds, or do you blame other people setting you off? (Remember the button is ours. No one can push a button unless we have it.)

Can you see how using the Three Spiritual Keys for Soulful Living will empower your life?

Can you identify experiences in your current life where you are not in alignment with love? If so, what action steps must you take to bring the relationship and your experience into alignment with love?

CHAPTER FIFTHTEEN

God IS Therefore I AM

I have shared my journey with you in hopes that you will begin to see that life itself is a mystical experience. I have also shared a few of my key teachings and tools that I believe when incorporated into your life will empower your life.

Every initiation/experience offers a life lesson and a gift. I know without a doubt that I AM who I was born to be. Thirty-four years ago I had no idea when I chose to end my marriage that I had arrived at a critical choice point in my life. I had no idea that I had been learning my life lessons through a vibrational signature that invited experiences of being a victim into my life. I didn't know that I was an incarnated soul. I didn't know that my soul and the world of spirit were communicating with me via my dreams, thought transmissions and my intuition.

Despite the not knowing, looking back, I can clearly see my soul and the world of spirit were guiding me. There was a path for me to follow. With every choice I made I had the power to change my life or not.

As I shared my story I can clearly see the critical choice points in my life as well as many of the initiations and activations I have received during the past thirty-four years. I can also see the times in my life I received what I call a God shot. A God shot temporarily awakens us to higher states of consciousness. It is up to each one of us when given a God shot to use the energy to empower our lives. God shots are experienced by many people as a surge of energy that allows them to change their life in major ways.

Today I fully embrace life as a modern day mystic.

As incarnated souls, I believe we are all mystics at heart. To seek God in every experience and activity is the quest of the mystic. I know that many spiritual teachers teach that mystical experiences are for the few, but I know that every day, ordinary people, have mystical experiences. To have a mystical experience is normal.

Many times a mystical experience simply shines the light on something we are experiencing and we see clearly. You begin to see life through the lens of spiritual consciousness and life takes on new meaning. I believe mystical experiences are missed by many personalities because they believe mystical experiences have to include angels, heavenly music, other worldly beings and out of body experiences. To the mystic a sunrise is a mystical experience. Looking into your lover's eyes is a mystical experience.

Life itself is the mystical experience. Tears flow as I wrote that last sentence because many people are missing why we are here on this planet.

Recently a student told me she can't claim that she is a mystic because people would think she is strange, or different.

I laughed at this because I always thought of myself as strange and different until I began teaching and found out that there are many people in this world just like me. I believe as we demystify what it means to be a mystic many people will begin to understand that they also *walk as one with God*.

God and I are not separated. God is not out there somewhere waiting for me to contact him. God IS, and EVERYTHING we experience is happening within God. The heart of the mystic knows that their heart is God's heart and their experiences are God's experience. There is no separation and there is nothing one has to do but open up and allow God to be experienced in one's life.

There are many pathways that can lead the student of soul to cultivating a deeper relationship with God and the world of spirit. As a teacher of soul the pathway I teach is simple. I have given you three spiritual keys to use as you create your experiences. The "Three Spiritual Keys for Empowered Soulful Living" puts you in charge of your life. The Three Spiritual Keys hold you responsible for that which you are creating at any given moment. The Three Spiritual Keys teach you that you are the creative force in your life; therefore, you must be mindful of that which you are creating.

Learn to be fully present in your life. Learn to see the initiations of your life as experiences that are seeking to shift you from living an unconscious life to a life that is fully experienced. As you move into a consciously created life you will begin to see the events and experiences that bring you to a critical choice point. When you arrive at these crossroads learn to ask for guidance from your soul and the world of spirit. Remember the path you choose at one of these crossroads will determine how and with whom you will learn your life lessons. None of the paths are wrong paths. The key difference is will you learn your life lessons by fire or with grace.

Mystics know that God is the only creative force, therefore I AM the creative force in my life. If we are unconscious of this truth, then you will not realize that everything you are experiencing you have created. To say that an experience has not met your expectations is to say God has not met your expectations. When you say that "I AM not enough" you are saying that God is not enough.

Everything we experience is occurring within God. There are many planes of consciousness within God, and our experience on earth is one of many planes of consciousness.

Nothing can exist without the spark of God in it.

The physical form cannot exist with the spark of God in it. If you see it, it has the spark of God in it. The same creative force that holds the chair together holds everything you experience together. God IS.

Many people think they have to do something like prayer to connect with God. The mystic understands that God is in every activity and experience. Ther e is no "reaching" out to God for the God that is "out there" is a man-made God. God IS. God is the experience, God is the energy, God IS.

God is a continued presence in my life. God is the continued presence in your life, even if you are not aware of this truth. God IS. We were all born having a steady stream of consciousness with God, and with the world of spirit. This steady stream of consciousness becomes blocked out as we are taught to focus on the outer world. Today begin to see your life through the eyes of the mystic.

Want to talk to God? Start right now by going to the mirror and saying hello. When you look into the mirror I guarantee you that God will be looking back at you.

Blessings, Katye Anna

About the Author

Katye Anna: For over twenty years, Katye Anna has been sharing her gifts and messages of transformation and empowered soulful living.

Katye Anna is a teacher of soul, transformational author, speaker, and workshop facilitator. Katye Anna embraces life as a mystical, magical, and spiritual journey; one she chooses to consciously walk with God. Katye Anna fully embodies the life of a modern day mystic.

Gifted with the ability to travel the many planes of consciousness within God, Katye Anna walks between worlds. Katye Anna has a direct connection to the world of soul and the world of spirit. Communicating with the world of spirit is as natural as breathing for Katye Anna.

Katye Anna writes and teaches from her heart and is guided by her soul, Anna, and spirit teachers. Her gifts of travel and sight allow her to do what many authors and spiritual teaches can't do - give firsthand descriptions of the many planes of consciousness within God.

When she writes about the tunnel of light, she writes from her firsthand accounts of helping people more into the light. When she writes about her sister Debbie's cabin in heaven, she can describe it in detail because she spends time with her there. When Katye Anna describes the Hall of Records where souls gather together to finalize soul agreements, she is describing it as she has seen it during her travels. Katye Anna uses her connection with the world of spirit to share the teachings of Anna. In 2013, Katye became the voice for Anna (thus the name Katye Anna). Anna is a group of 976 souls who no longer experience consciousness on earth. Anna teaches from the higher planes of consciousness and seeks to bring forth teachings that will help personalities take responsibility for the energy they bring to earth and their experiences.

The insight from Anna is endless. Katye Anna's books offer teachings and guidance meant to help shift people's awareness about being incarnated souls.

Further, her work illustrates how our experiences here on earth are just a small part of the journey of the soul. Katye Anna provides teachings and experiences to help clients and students release old outdated beliefs and patterns. Once that is accomplished, they are able to lead empowered lives fueled by one's soul and the universe. Together with Anna, Katye teaches students and clients how to consciously connect with their own soul.

Katye Anna believes everyone has a direct line to the world of spirit. Through meditations and spiritual guidance, Katye Anna opens those she works with to embrace their own unique line of communication with the world of spirit. With her messages of love, she seeks to show that everyone can live an empowered life.

Information

For information about Katye Anna's ongoing classes and events go to: *www.KatyeAnna.com*

To contact Katye Anna for speaking engagements write to: *Katye@katyeanna.com*

What to sign up for a Mind Mastery Class go to: katyeanna. com/mind
To find out more information about Katye Anna's Next Life Mastery Year Long Program go to: katyeanna.com/life

Join Katye Anna on Facebook at:
https://www.facebook.com/KatyeAnna

Other books written by Katye Anna:

"Birthing into Spirit" for more information go to: *http://birthingintospiritbook.com/*

"Conscious Construction of the Soul" for more information go to: *http://consciousconstructionbook.com*

"Soul Love Never Ends"for more information go to: http://katyeanna.com/soul

If you would like to give a review for *CrossRoads- Living A Soul Inspired Life* please visit Amazon.com. Go to *CrossRoads – Living A Soul Inspired Life* by Katye Anna click the button that says, "Write a customer review". Thank-you for your support.

Made in the USA
Columbia, SC
06 November 2017